SPORTSMAN'S
BEST

BOOK & DVD SERIES

FS Books:

Sportsman's Best: Inshore Fishing
Sportsman's Best: Offshore Fishing
Sportsman's Best: Snapper & Grouper
Sportsman's Best: Sailfish
Sportsman's Best: Redfish

Sport Fish of Florida
Sport Fish of the Gulf of Mexico
Sport Fish of the Atlantic
Sport Fish of Fresh Water
Sport Fish of the Pacific

Baits, Rigs & Tackle
Annual Fishing Planner
The Angler's Cookbook

Florida Sportsman Magazine
Shallow Water Angler Magazine
Florida Sportsman Fishing Charts
Lawsticks
Law Boatstickers

Author, Terry Lacoss
Edited by Terry Gibson and Florida Sportsman Staff
Art Director, Drew Wickstrom
Illustrations by Joe Suroviec
Copy Edited by Sam Hudson
Photos by Scott Sommerlatte, Joe Richard, Pat Ford, David McCleaf,
MirrOlure and Stinson & Partners, Inc., Kendall Osborne and FS Staff

First Printing
ISBN: 1-892947-90-0

www.floridasportsman.com

REDFISH

CONTENTS

SPORTSMAN'S BEST
R E D F I S H

44

84

166

Nothing like seeing your tail on the cover of a national magazine. This Larry Kinder image of a redfish tailing in marsh grass made the cover of *Shallow Water Angler*.

Look at Mister Redfish Now

My first hunt for redfish "bonefish style" was done vicariously in 1982. There on the 19-inch Zenith was a guy poling an angler for tailing redfish, of all things.

I was into bonefishing by then, but fished for reds the "usual" way, bumping shrimp-tipped jigs around oyster bars in the Everglades backcountry. Having yet to sight fish for reds, I was riveted to the screen.

That segment of Outdoor Life was filmed in Florida Bay, out of Flamingo, and the guide was Miami's Capt. Skip Soulé. Skip still guides out of Flamingo, and is of the old guard, having stalked flats reds when that fishery was in its infancy. Skip is calm and patient, as a flats guide should be. Good thing, because his celebrity angler was NFL defensive end Mark Gastineau, 280 pounds of muscle with not an ounce of sight-fishing experience. This New York Jets player was known for his "sack dance," which he gleefully performed over squashed quarterbacks. Just as Skip pioneered flats redfishing, Gastineau pioneered on-the-field showboating, both of which have become art forms today. Thanks to Skip's expertise, big Mark eventually hooked a few tailers. Thankfully, he did not dance on the skiff. That might have even gotten a rise out of Skip.

That footage opened my eyes to a new brand of redfishing. I dove into it soon thereafter, at Flamingo.

"Man, there's ol' Mister Redfish now!" I remember whispering to my dad, when I spotted that first tail. I would've never believed it. From that point on, sight fishing for reds cut into my bonefishing time. They are easier to catch, tail more vigorously, and unlike bonefish, reds forgive an occasional bad cast. They'll even give you a second shot, sometimes a third. Reds fast-tracked my saltwater fly-fishing development. I felt they were the perfect flats fish. And I still do.

Needless to say, word got out. Fast forward to 2007. Over southern Atlantic and Gulf shallows, Mister Redfish drives the sight-fishing passion. The once-lowly red drum has risen to superstar status.

So, why all this fuss over a drum?

It's simple. Reds are more widely distributed than any other flats gamefish species. They eat readily, fight hard and taste great. Reds have injected new life into the flats skiff and saltwater, light-tackle industry. That lofty stature demands that we all do our utmost to conserve what is fast becoming the most vital gamefish on southern inshore waters. And, what do you say we respect the fish's environs and fellow anglers' space while we're at it?

"Sportsman's Best: Redfish" is a tribute to the species and to past conservation successes. Written by Terry Lacoss and edited by *Florida Sportsman* Projects Editor Terry Gibson and the FS staff, it is the most thorough reference ever compiled on fishing for redfish. Enjoy.

—Mike Conner, Editor, *Shallow Water Angler* magazine

It is vital that we ... ... are
... ... will be redfish for future
generations ... ... This
young man is clearly hooked...

Introduction
A Lifetime of Redfishing

T he first place I caught a redfish was in a narrow tidal creek that when flooded, almost makes its way to the back porch of Florida's Amelia Island Plantation golf pro shop. It's a place I revisited time and again, while giving golf lessons for a living. At lunchtime, I would load a cart with fishing gear and drive to one of the deep turns in the creek. Slowly hopping a plastic tail on a ¼-ounce jig did the trick. The fight from a 5- to 10-pound redfish was better than most fights I had experienced in other kinds of fishing.

Later, on my days off, I began to put clients on redfish from the Amelia Links golf pro shop. I had my guiding information posted over the golf shop's drinking fountain for resort guests to see. The signs were more than advertisements; they were signs of one obsession supplanting another. Wondering if I had condemned myself to a life of poverty, in 1978 I turned down a head golf pro job in Atlanta, Georgia, to become Amelia Island Plantation's "Fishing Director." But I knew I'd miss Mr. Redfish too much if I moved inland, and "Fishing Director" seemed a mighty fine title to me.

During my 30-year career, I have put clients on a variety of both fresh- and saltwater species, but my favorite gamefish of all still remains the hard-fighting redfish. I often wondered why the species didn't have more of a following. Then, in the late '90s, redfishing became so popular that tournament trails emerged. This gave me the opportunity to travel with my son, Terry David, to waters that we had never fished before. Catching redfish in different waters became a new challenge, one we both pursued with new energy. But tournaments aren't for everyone, and nothing beats a day of fishing alone, or with close friends and family just for fun.

I remain fascinated by how redfish will take a variety of lures, including spinners, hard baits, surface lures and flies. Fortunately, my home waters in Northeast Florida harbor a wide variety of redfish habitats that call for a variety of tactics, from deep jigging for bull reds at the St. Marys Inlet, to wade fishing for tailing reds in the flooded spartina grassflats. I've never stopped learning, and neither, I suspect, will you.

—Terry Lacoss

CHAPTER 1

The Ultimate Gamefish

Redfish were long considered a "blue collar" species, or just a good candidate for the cooler. It's hard to understand why that reputation persisted, or why gamefish status, in the legal and figurative meanings of the term, took so long. The species is challenging to catch, good to eat and stunning to behold, in its own quirky way. Their bodies are almost paradoxical.

The big head and brawny neck and shoulders belong to a powerful, aggressive predator; the tail to a clever, swift and strikingly beautiful animal. The spot or spots are thought to represent "eyes," to fool larger predators into striking at a fleet tail. No one knows how or why the blue accents on the tail evolved, but pure ornamentation is a distinct possibility. Our respect for this fish is evident in our efforts to protect stocks and habitats, and of course in our passion for pursuing them.

The head and brawny shoulders belong to a powerful, aggressive predator; the tail to a clever, swift and strikingly beautiful animal.

See DVD for more on the ultimate gamefish.

It starts with a tail waving on a shallow
flat, and winds down as a furious tail
churning away from a skiff for the last
time. Either way, the tails have it.

Southland Celebrities

A school of Louisiana spawning bull redfish darkens the glass-slick surface of the Gulf of Mexico.

A teal-tinted bronze tail waves between strands of Georgia spartina grass.

A marauding band of fish turns a green, Outer Banks wave bronze.

A push of water moves through Florida mangrove shoots.

Red drum (*Sciaenops ocellatus*), or "redfish," or occasionally "channel bass" inhabit almost every kind of coastal habitat from Delaware Bay and occasionally northward, south to the Florida Keys and throughout inshore waters of the Gulf of Mexico. Cuba and northeastern Mexico also have populations of redfish. But the species receives little attention abroad, compared to the United States, where it now enjoys celebrity status. According to surveys by the National Marine Fisheries Service (NMFS) and private research firm Southwick

During the fall, full moon tides flood Low Country marshes and give reds acce

Associates, only striped bass (*Morone saxatilis*) and speckled trout (*Cynoscion nebulosus*) are more popular among U.S. saltwater anglers.

Their popularity is understandable. Redfish are eager feeders, and they fight like bulldogs. In fact, I have frequently watched in amazement as a hooked redfish swims straight back into a school, behaving as if it had never felt the hook, or the pressure of the deeply bent rod.

Redfish are also, of course, delicious. Unfortunately, their firm white meat nearly did them in, during the blackened redfish craze of the 1980s. They're also quite beautiful, and fascinating, in terms of their life histories and anatomy. What anglers seem to love most about the species is the sheer number and types of places where you can catch them, and the variety of techniques you can use to catch them. If you learned to fish exclusively for redfish, you would still master an astounding array of waters, gear and techniques.

Accessibility factors heavily into the redfish's popularity. You can put as much or as little effort and expense into redfishing as you like, and still stand a good chance of eating redfish on a half shell that night. Sometimes, especially if the fish are spooky or hard hit, simple wading is the most effective way to catch fish. Hardcore flats fishermen and tournament anglers maintain costly skiffs and bay boats in order to cover lots of water, but some days the most productive flats may be right next to the boat ramp.

Others build tricked-out surf fishing vehicles. In North Carolina, surf fishermen have the opportunity to land world records while

o a favorite forage source, fiddler crabs.

Abundant redfish keep anglers happy from southernmost Texas waters to the Chesapeake Bay and occasionally parts farther north.

fishing from the back of a pickup truck, or while wetting waders in pounding surf. When David Deuel caught his world-record red drum, he was doing just that, enjoying a late fall surf fishing trip on foot. The record redfish, caught in 1984 off an Outer Banks beach, weighed 94 pounds, 2 ounces. Redfishing can happen anywhere in salt water, brackish estuaries and at times, in fresh water. Redfish can be caught from bridges, in inlets, around jetties, around oysters heads, on seagrass-covered flats, on spartina flats, and on offshore live bottom. There are even a couple of golf course ponds

suing a school of redfish on a shallow flat, either on foot or in a glass slipper of a poling skiff. Of all the places where you can sight fish for reds, perhaps none are more challenging than flooded spartina grassflats. You become a hunter, as you stalk redfish by watching for their tails to pop through the surface. You take aim, and must make the fly or lure land in a circle no bigger than a bull's-eye, and land gently at that. If the fish eats and you hook up, there's still the matter of pulling the fish out of the jungle. Once your quarry finds thick vegetation, it begins to tangle your line and

where I live on Amelia Island, Florida, that are full of them.

It's clear that redfish haunt a lot of very different places, but for many anglers the biggest thrill comes when stalking a large school in shallow water. In the world of fishing, nothing is more exciting than pur-

leader, often resulting in a dislodged hook, or a parted line. It's the kind of fight that every fisherman should experience at least once in his lifetime.

Most redfish enthusiasts own a diverse quiver of rods and reels, including spinning tackle, baitcasters, fly rods and perhaps surf sticks. Spinning tackle is best suited for throwing light soft-plastic baits and jigs. Fly tackle gives you a stealth advantage when the fish are shallow and spooky. You can't beat a baitcaster for accuracy and drag strength, or for freelining live baits. In fact, there's a lot of crossover among bass anglers, because "bass" tackle and tactics work really well, with slight modifications, for redfish. The spoon, for instance, has been a favorite among bass anglers for more than a century, and in some areas it is the number one lure for redfish, too.

Redfish are generally cooperative, compared to bonefish, permit, and big trout and snook laid up shallow. For one thing, they can withstand dramatic changes in water

species of saltwater gamefish have migrated to deeper water and developed a case of lockjaw, redfish stick around.

Fishermen will generally find that redfish school according to generations, or by size, but there are surprises. It's not uncommon to locate a school of redfish weighing one to two pounds and minutes later discover a school of giants weighing from 20 to 35 pounds. Florida's Mosquito Lagoon is one of those unique fisheries.

Fishing for redfish is growing in popularity by leaps and bounds, particularly in southern states where the species can be found schooling on shallow flats. This style of fishing can be enjoyed from Texas to North Carolina, where inlets and bays give way to

Left, a team of anglers works a Northeast Florida oyster bar. Above, the jackpot. Thanks to the twin relatively large holes in front of each eye, a red drum has an amazingly keen sense of smell. The holes are called "nares."

temperature, on both the cold and the warm ends. Even on a winter's day when the wind is blowing hard from the north and the water is choppy, muddy and cold, redfish are always willing to feed and put up a fight. They'll eat when they're hot, too. They just don't like to have to travel far for a meal. But when other

shallow marshes, grassflats and bars. Perhaps, like me, you'll be captivated by stalking those big redfish on shallow flats, feeding with their noses in the bottom and their tails in the air. But know that there a thousand other places to catch what is arguably the ultimate inshore gamefish. SB

CHAPTER 2

The Redfish

The scientific name for redfish is *Sciaenops ocellatus*. *Sciaenops*, a generic word for "perch-like" fish, is a derivative of the Greek family name for the drums, which is *Sciaenidae*. *Ocellatus* is a Latin word meaning "oscillated," or "spotted," due to the prominent spot or spots on the backs and tails of the species. Common names for redfish include redfish, red drum, rat red, bull red, spot-tail bass, channel bass and just "red."

Redfish are part of a very large and very old family of fishes. Sixty million years ago, the species' direct ancestors evolved into the first spiny ray fishes, which were the earliest relatives of striped bass and snook. On this present bank and shoal of time, red drum cohabitate with their close relatives the speckled trout *(Cynoscion nebulosus)*, weakfish *(Cynoscion regalis)*, black drum *(Pogonias cromis)*, whiting *(Menticirrhus americanus)*, various croakers, and spot *(Leiostomus xanthurus)*. There are also suites of Pacific, South Atlantic and Indian Ocean drums.

Good eyesight, a strong sense of smell, keen hearing and a sensitive lateral line make redfish a tough adversary to stalk.

Scott Sommerlatte
A membrane over the retina called
the *tapetum lucidum* allows
redfish to see well in low light.

The Art of Redfish

Whether tailing in soft, early morning light, snaking through mangrove props or pouncing on forage, red drum tantalize the mind's eye. We thought you might enjoy some different styles of artistic expression, while reading about what makes redfish so fascinating. A better understanding of their life cycle is the key to safe management and conservation.

Brian Sylvester
Feeding reds pique the interest
of a roseate spoonbill.

Habitat Preferences

The life history of a fish is described by scientists as its ontogenetic developement.

Catch a drum, and you'll quickly understand why they're named after a musical instrument. The males of most drum species use extrinsic muscles around their swim bladders to make a drumming sound. (The exception is the black drum, the most recently evolved of the family. Both male and female black drum make sounds, and actually carry on quite a conversation when preparing to spawn.) Big tides, water temperature and the length of the day tell redfish when to spawn. During the fall, when the days shorten and the water temperatures begin to drop, redfish feel the urge to get busy.

During the spawn, mature male redfish drum to attract nearby female redfish. It has also been observed in hatcheries that male redfish change to a dark red color when mating. The male redfish then nudges the stomach of the female redfish by poking its head into the female's abdomen, perhaps to both excite the female and to encourage her to release her eggs.

Once the eggs are dispersed by female redfish, the males fertilize the eggs and the eggs then float to the surface. Unfertilized eggs sink to the bottom and become food for crabs and other benthic (bottom-dwelling) organisms. Following fertilization, the redfish embryo immediately begins to develop inside the egg. Larvae hatch in less than 32 hours, especially if the water temperature is in the neighborhood of 72 degrees.

Three days after hatching, the mouth, stomach, intestines and liver are formed. The organism is about .007 of an inch in length.

Then, for three more days, yolk in the egg sack provides nourishment. After that, baby food for redfish larvae consists of a variety of plankton.

Over the next three to six weeks, larvae remain incredibly vulnerable. In fact, less than one percent of newly hatched redfish will survive to become adults. Many larvae become food for other critters, or drift into areas devoid of vital habitats.

As larvae and as post-larval fish, red drum are also terribly susceptible to poor water quality. Indeed, just because anglers routinely catch adult redfish in compromised waterways such as

Helterskeletons.com
Skeleton mount of red drum.

Florida's Caloosahatchee or St. Lucie rivers, does not mean the fishery will remain healthy. Adult fish can swim away from discharges of runoff and other pollution events. And within certain thresholds, they can withstand relatively powerful and sudden doses of dirty fresh water and other pollutants compared to most other gamefish. As adults, they're one tough fish. But too much poor water and habitat loss, and year class after year class of redfish larvae and older juveniles never "graduate."

Redfish larvae rely on tides and local currents to sweep them into seagrass meadows, marshes and shallow creeks, which serve as nurseries. But the larvae do exhibit a fairly high degree of motility. During a high flood tide, redfish larvae swim to the surface and ride the strong incoming flows. This is also done at night when they are less visible to predators. During the daytime hours, redfish larvae swim deep where silt and other particles disguise their presence. Larvae also swim to the bottom during a falling tide. Tidal currents weaken as you go deeper and are stronger on the surface of an incoming tide. By staying

Joe Suroviec
Lone mangroves hold
finfish forage.

deep during the falling tide and swimming close to the surface on an incoming tide, red-fish larvae increase the odds of arriving in nurseries

The waters where larval and post-larval fish spend their next stages of development are called "settling areas." Again, ideal settling and nursery waters include shallow marsh creeks with Spartina and other grasses, and/or oysters for cover. Once in these nurseries, red-fish larvae will transform into juvenile redfish.

Post-larval redfish quickly become "oscillated," or spotted. Scientists hypothesize that the large black spot or spots located on the backs and tails of redfish resembles an eye or eyes. The spot(s) is a means of defense, fooling

predators into striking at the tail of the redfish, instead of the head, and thus allowing a speedy escape. It's not uncommon for redfish, especially juveniles, to have multiple black spots on their tail and sides. Again, scientists think that multiple spots serve to confuse predators about the location of the head. They may also camouflage juveniles against the bottom, making it harder for predatory birds to spot them.

That very few large adult redfish keep multiple spots seems to indicate that redfish become less vulnerable to predation as they grow larger. Redfish can live up to 25 years and reach a length of 60 inches and weigh as much as 94 pounds. Females can release as many as 3.5 million eggs per spawning event.

Red drum are predominantly bottom feeders, and very effective bottom feeders at that, due to their underslung jaws. They have to be effective feeders, or else they could not support such phenomenal growth rates, an evolutionary adaptation that gives them several advantages over slow-growing fish such as groupers. By growing 11 to 12 inches in length during their first year and attaining a weight of up to one pound, redfish hurtle through those early life stages where they are most vulnerable to predation. Given optimal environmental conditions, subadult redfish can grow to 31 inches in four years and attain weights up to 12 pounds. They also reach sexual maturity relatively quickly, which makes sub-populations of the species less likely to disappear entirely from overfishing with harmful gear such as gillnets, or from marine diseases such as red tides or those caused by human pollution. Survival, quite simply, is a numbers game. However, upon reaching sexual maturity, the growth rate slows considerably.

The largest recorded redfish have come from the Carolina coastlines. David G. Deuel holds the International Game Fish Association (IGFA) all-tackle record. He caught a 94-pound, 2-ounce redfish on November 7, 1984, in North Carolina's Outer Banks. A.J. Taylor holds the South Carolina state record, of 75 pounds, which he caught in 1965 during a fishing trip to Murrell's Inlet.

To catch redfish regularly, you have to use a wide variety of lures, flies and baits, because the species' diet varies dramatically throughout its life history, even long before they reach targetable size. As ½-inch to 3½-inch fingerlings, grass shrimp, opossum shrimp and copepods comprise 95 percent of their diet. These forage sources offer an incredible amount of protein for their size. Once the fingerling reds

Steve Whitlock
Along many coasts, pinfish are favorite redfish forage.

Jim Roberts
Fish rubbing.

attain a size of 3½ to 7 inches, their diet becomes more pisciverous. It shifts to 60 percent fish and 40 percent grass shrimp, mud crabs and fiddler crabs. Their diet changes again when they reach a length of 21 inches—back to 60 percent fiddler crabs, swimming crabs, mud crabs and grass shrimp. At that size, fish make up only around 35 percent of their diet, which says volumes about the forage available in the habitats that young redfish prefer, such as spartina flats and mangroves. It's also a cue for the angler in terms of selection of flies and lures in those habitats.

Mature redfish, those measuring over 21

beaches, shoals and offshore livebottom. And even juvenile redfish can tolerate a wide range of salinity levels. According to biologist Jim Davis, they can tolerate salinity levels as low as 13 parts per trillion (ppt) and as high as 40 ppt. (Florida's St. Johns River is an excellent example, where redfish can be found at rock jetties at the mouth of the Atlantic, and 100 miles upstream in fresh water.)

Marshland tidal creeks are of critical importance for redfish from the time they settle to maturity. Newly hatched redfish are biologically obligated to shallow tidal marsh creeks. The vast spartina or "cordgrass" marshlands of the Low Country and Northeast Florida, especially those located close to major inlet mouths, are the most productive nursery grounds for young redfish in that region. Proximity to near-

Redfish are better equipped as bottom feeders, but often forage on a variety of baitfish. They're especially fond of pilchards.

inches, feed more on fishes than do smaller reds, but there's a tremendous amount of regional and seasonal variations in their dietary preferences. Menhaden, mullet, croaker and spots are often found in the stomachs of adult redfish. But I once witnessed a shark fisherman catch and release a 25-pound bull red, while fishing with a 3-pound bluefish. Apparently, few meals are too big for a hungry adult redfish.

Having a good understanding of redfish habitat preferences will increase your fishing success. Broadly speaking, that includes coastal rivers, marshlands and bay areas,

by inlets allows for easy access. Any time the transport distance to the nursery is reduced, survival rate increases. There's simply less exposure time to predators and pollutants. Juvenile redfish also demonstrate a preference for grassy marshes and creeks all along the Gulf Coast.

In shallow marshes and marsh creeks, redfish take advantage of two major factors. First and foremost, shallow creeks provide a refuge from large and hungry fish. Secondly, appropriately sized food is abundant. Falling tides carry food from the marshes to shallow creek pools.

In winter, deepwater refuges become impor-

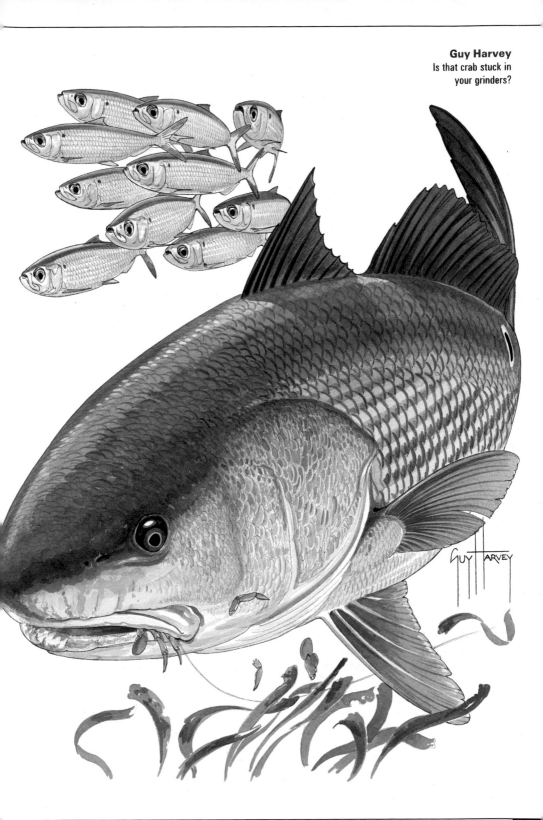

Guy Harvey
Is that crab stuck in
your grinders?

tant for juvenile redfish. Plummeting water temperatures often force young reds from these shallow marsh creeks to nearby deep channels. Adults head there, too. But studies have shown that young juvenile redfish do not grow during the winter season, and in some cases, even lose body weight. Winter's a tough time for them.

Sometime between the ages of 10 and 12 months, subadult redfish move from the shallow creeks out into the main rivers, larger creeks and shallow grassflats. Large shallow flats offer excellent habitat for pre-adult redfish, particularly when bordering marshlands or mangrove tree shorelines provide nearby cover. These shallow flats are also more attractive to redfish if they are near deep channels, creeks or rivers. Biologists calls these areas "deepwater refugia." Slightly deeper depressions in the bottom make them

highly attractive, too. Shallow, mudbottom flats that support submerged vegetation, such as seagrasses, are essential. Large sand holes located on a fairly large grassflat are particularly attractive to schooling redfish. Typically these large sand holes are slightly deeper than nearby grassflats, where the falling tides gather both forage foods and hungry reds.

The situation is a little different in southernmost Florida, where redfish inhabit mangrove forests. Here, redfish can live in a maze of mangrove roots and find both forage and protection from predators. Small crustaceans and a variety of other tiny creatures can be found clinging to mangrove roots, and that in turn attracts baitfish and crabs, all of which are delicacies for foraging redfish. Mangrove edges adjacent to grassflats, oys-

Randy McGovern
Crab Crazy, race to the cork.

ter bars or small tidal creeks are most attractive to redfish.

In terms of behavior, redfish are definitely a schooling gamefish, and they school in size classes, according to generation. When they reach sexual maturity, redfish schools migrate out into the open waters of the nearby Gulf or Atlantic. Mature redfish range in sizes from 10 to over 30 pounds and will live in water as deep as 50 feet. During the fall, major spawns take place at inlet mouths, beaches and bays where redfish go on serious feeding sprees. During this time of the year, it's not unusual for fishermen to catch and release 30 to 50 bull redfish during a good tide. The best tide is the last of the flood when the water is clear, setting up perfect spawning conditions.

Pigmentation

On some flats, redfish look dark as logs. Others, they are almost as silvery and reflective as bonefish. In general, the colors range from a bright copper red to a silvery shade of copper. The back of a redfish is typically darker in color and the stomach an off-white color. Redfish that live in clear water are a silver-copper color. In stained water, redfish develop bright copper-red sides.

Redfish will also change their colors when holding over a clean sand

bottom, to blend in. Redfish that hold a short distance away in the back of a bay filled with clean water and vegetation will sport a deep,

copper-red color. Reds that live in brackish water will obtain a deep, orange-red. A good example of this drastic color change from a sil-

very-copper color to "goldfish" takes place in Louisiana "duck ponds." Here bayous run for miles back into the marsh, often opening up

Rob Chapman
Redfish tailing on a shrimp.

into large freshwater ponds. These ultra-clear ponds support a variety of freshwater vegetation and brilliantly orange painted redfish, which turn silver as they migrate toward the open Gulf.

Predators

Besides humans, the porpoise is the adult redfish's number one enemy. Schools of porpoises often surround a school of redfish. Once the school is corralled into a tight pod, one by one the porpoises take turns feeding, often tossing redfish six feet in the air before eating them.

A variety of sharks also feed on redfish. Catch-and-release can make reds even more vulnerable. (I once secured a 6-pound redfish with my set of mechanical lip grabbers and was about to lift the red into the boat, when I spotted a large bull shark. The 6-foot shark vaulted from the water, landing headfirst on top of my redfish with snapping jaws and only inches from my hand. Within a few seconds, there was nothing left of the redfish, except for a pool of blood.)

Such porpoise and shark attacks give good reason why redfish live in a shallow water world. Under full attack, redfish typically retreat to the shallow edge of the flat.

During one such attack, porpoises attacked some 200 redfish. They succeeded in surprising the school and several reds were eaten right in front of our eyes. The survivors raced onto the nearby flat. They ran so high and dry their backs poked out the water, as they lay side by side almost on dry land. After the porpoises had left, the reds soon returned to the nearby sand hole and grassflat. SB

Jean Eastman
The location of the eyes, nares and mouth helps reds find food in grass.

Carey Chen
A flat is a city with different citizens providing important functions. Mullet and crabs housekeep and provide protein for reds, sheepshead and birds.

Carey Chen ©

CHAPTER 3

Evolution of a Fishery

A fishery includes the targeted species as well as the community that fishes for the individual species. Fortunately, most states where red drum occur have given them "gamefish" status, meaning that red drum cannot be commercially harvested or sold. Some states have also banned gillnetting, a practice that nearly wiped out redfish in many areas on both the Atlantic and Gulf coasts.

Finally, sound, fair and scientifically derived size and catch limits are mostly in place, but there is always room for improvement. By joining the Coastal Conservation Association or other fishing-friendly conservation groups, and by being a conscientious boater, you can help maintain a sustainable fishery.

The '80s blackened redfish craze put a premium on redfish fille Conservation-minded magazines and the CCA saved the fishery by lobbying successfully for gamefish status in key states.

To call redfish a denizen of shallow water is an understatement. They spend a good portion of their lives with their backs and tails in the air.

Red Drum: A Cause Célèbre

While redfish have always been a staple, they haven't been a celebrity species for all that long. Throughout the 1970s and '80s, speckled trout were definitely the most sought after inshore gamefish. According to a recent study, speck-led trout remain the most targeted inshore saltwater fish in their range. But there's a lot of regional variation in that assessment. Many places, redfish are king.

The story of the redfish's evolution from meat fish to prized gamefish is fascinating. Many shallow-water anglers were more interested in pursuing fish that were either much easier or much harder to catch. In fact, Outer Banks surf fishermen were one of the few subcultures that really made a point of targeting reds. But anglers looking for steady action and a sure-fire fish dinner drifted live shrimp under long, slender and brilliantly colored floats for trout, occasionally tying into a redfish. In South Florida, sight-fishing fanatics focused on bonefish, permit and tarpon. Pioneer flats fishermen in the Florida Keys took shots at reds incidentally, but few ever left the dock specifically in search of them. But some angling celebrities realized that the species has a unique allure. The redfish's rise in popularity among Florida anglers began partly because the bonefish/permit/tarpon elite gradually began targeting them.

Florida Sportsman Senior Editor Vic Dunaway explains that, "sight fishing for redfish had originally sprung up in the Keys as an offshoot of bonefishing. For years, the guides just took their redfish as they happened to find them while bonefishing."

Dunaway recalls that by the late '60s, sight fishing for reds "was a firmly entrenched activity but confined to Florida Bay."

Pioneer flats fishermen incidentally took shots at reds while searching for bonefish, permit and tarpon.

Al Pflueger Jr., pioneering sight fishing on the Indian River Lagoon.

The biggest driver of the rise in popularity has been the excitement of sight fishing for tailing reds.

Scott Deal, president of Maverick Boat Company, explained that, "The style of fishing, where teams of two anglers pole across the flats sight fishing owned the romance, the celebrity and excitement of inshore fishing. Legends such as Al Pflueger Jr. started targeting redfish the same way, and suddenly people started thinking a lot differently about redfish. Now, folks are buying skiffs and getting into sight fishing just about everywhere that redfish swim."

"It's sight fishing—the visual aspect—that turned redfish from a plain ole 'grass carp' to a celebrity species here in Texas, and in other Gulf states," said Capt. Bruce Shuler, who has fished Texas' Lower Laguna Madre since the '50s. Shuler explained that redfish were never unappreciated, but that trout were the primary

targets through the '70s.

"Trout were the fish we went after. We kept reds if we caught 'em, but trout were the fish we were after."

In Texas and other Gulf states, the adage "you don't know what you've got 'til it's gone" almost proved true. Shuler recalls that by the '70s, there were so few redfish left in Texas bays that few anglers targeted them.

"But we sure cared enough about them to fight the redfish wars in the '70's, when the commercial sector nearly netted redfish into extinction," said Shuler.

"Commercial fishermen blocked roads, violence ensued. Almost everything short of gun play went down. But we won, and commercial harvest of redfish was banned in Texas. A trophy trout is still worth more than a trophy red

Redfish are never abundant enough, but in most areas healthy reds like this one are common catches. Above, Capt. Bruce Shuler (pictured) and son Brandon are two of the most important voices in Texas conservation.

here. But the level of enthusiasm for redfish is incredible."

Ironically, putting redfish in the limelight also helped save the species from collapse in Florida and the other Gulf states. Commercial overfishing was rampant during the '80s blackened redfish craze. The recreational fishing community's passion for the species was channeled into several landmark conservation victories, including gamefish status for the species and gillnet bans in a number of states. (To learn more about redfish conservation, turn to Chapter 17.) But long before the species teetered on the brink of collapse, enthusiasm

Bob Hewes is credited for building the first pure-bred flats skiff, and the firs

for redfishing sparked major design innovations in skinny-running skiffs. In fact, the Florida Bay fishery gave rise to the first skiff ever designed specifically to catch redfish.

Very few boats at the time were designed to draw less than 12 inches. Those that drew less were specialty boats built to fish the shallow

skiff designed specifically for redfishing.

South Florida flats for permit, tarpon and bonefish. According to Vic Dunaway, pioneers such as Al Pflueger Jr., Bill Curtis and Stu Apte ran a brand called a FiberCraft, one of the first boats to make use of fiberglass. Before that, flats skiffs were "either self-rigged or built locally." In the early days, some companies, such as Pro-Line, already manufactured fishing boats with flat bottoms to fish the shallow waters of the Gulf. But Bob Hewes is credited for building the first pure-bred flats skiff, the Bonefisher. He would also become the first builder to develop a shallow-draft skiff specifically for redfishing.

In the early '70s, legendary angler Al Pflueger Jr. took Bob Hewes redfishing out front of Flamingo.

"I was trying to get him to make a lighter

During the blackened redfish craze, commercial fishermen literally bailed the spawning stock of reds into bins and off to markets. Above, an early iteration of a flats skiff, and cooler for casting platform.

boat, one without an inner liner, and one that would only need a smaller outboard, so we could float shallower," recalls Pflueger.

"I poled him until I could pole no further, but to where he could see these reds wallowing in inches of water. I got him where he could see the fish but couldn't get to them. So, Hewes went back to the factory, stripped down the Bonefisher, and developed the Redfisher."

The rising popularity also caused a re-birth of sorts for the "bay boat," slightly larger, generally center console vessels that draw more

> **The challenge now is to fish responsibly, respecting the grassflats and other habitats.**

water than flats skiffs, but handle a family and chop much better. (Turn to Chapter 5, for more info on boats.)

It became a sporting challenge for fishermen to navigate shallow-water flats with their skinny-water fishing boats. Some even bragged back on land how shallow they floated. It got downright competitive, and redfish divisions became an important intrinsic part of major tournaments such as the Miami Met. Later, redfish tournaments styled after largemouth bass tournaments and circuits emerged.

Redfish tournaments began a new era in competitive fishing during the late 1980s. One of the first redfish tours was promoted by the Inshore Fisherman's Association, out of Jacksonville, Florida. Today there are several redfish tournament trails, including the Oh Boy! Oberto Redfish Cup and the FLW redfish tours, all of which offer big money and nationally televised action. They say everyone gets their 15 minutes of fame, and thanks to televised tournaments, there are a lot of famous redfish swimming around.

Indeed, television has played a role in promoting redfishing and creating celebrity status for the species. Televised fishing shows also began showcasing many areas of the coastal waters, such as the Low Country marshes, where redfish were thought of more as a "channel bass" than a flats dweller. Viewers who didn't even enjoy fishing, began watching the televised shows simply because of the beautiful coastal settings in which the shows were filmed. And viewers learned that they could sight fish and apply the more technical approaches to redfishing in their home waters.

It's great that so many folks have learned to love redfish. The challenge now is to fish responsibly, minding the limits, respecting the grassflats and other habitats, and spreading the ethic. SB

Tournament circuits including the IFA and FLA tours promote redfishing, as do television shows such as Shallow Water Angler.

Thanks in part to redfish the kayak fleet
has grown exponentially. Jenny McBride
often kayaks with dad, Jerry in the Stuart,
Florida area. This red's pretty big for the
southern Indian River Lagoon.

CHAPTER 4

Tackle

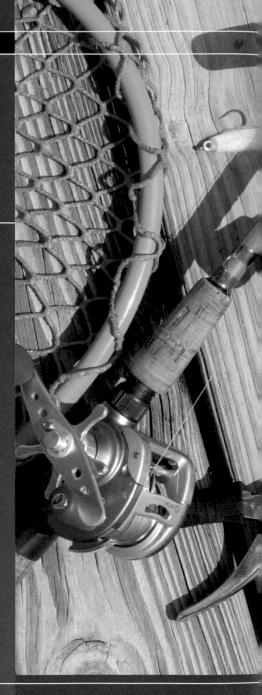

To optimize opportunities and fun, a "Renaissance" fisherman masters the spinning rod, the plug rod and the fly rod.

Spinning rods are best for beginners, as they are the easiest to cast. Spinning rods are also best suited for throwing light live baits such as shrimp and crabs, and light soft-plastic baits. Generally, they're the least likely to cause problems when casting into the wind. But, it's hard to beat a baitcasting or "plug" rod for control, especially when working a shoreline with a topwater. Baitcasting rods are pretty tough to beat in terms of casting distance, too, when fan casting a jig on a big flat.

Fly tackle is mostly about finesse, about making a pinpoint presentation to an individual fish on a skinny flat. But a good fly caster can work pockets along shorelines as accurately and stealthily as a dart shooter, and at times out-fish more conventional methods.

A good philosophy about redfishing tackle might be, "Match the horse to the course."

See DVD for more on using your whole arsenal.

There are so many tools for reds
that you get to play with a
diverse array of really fun toys.

The Full Quiver

Dating back at least to the 19th century, revolving spool baitcasting or "plug" reels were in wide use long before spinning tackle became available. A plug casting outfit is a timeless tool for redfish. In Texas and in other regions along the Gulf of Mexico, many anglers use plug tackle exclusively. You

Plug tackle has been slaying red drum dating back to the 19th century.

can stop the revolving spool with thumb pressure instantly, allowing for pinpoint casts. With a heavy enough lure, good plug tackle will out-distance spinning tackle. Drags are generally stronger, and you have the added advantage of being able to apply drag instantly with your thumb.

Fly fishermen were long viewed by those on the outside looking in as elite (and elitist)

anglers looking to handicap themselves to make redfishing even more sporting. However, in the right hands there is no deadlier tool when sight fishing for spooky reds on super skinny flats, or for sight fishing for tailers in spartina grass. You can present a highly imitative pattern much more softly and more accurately with a fly rod. And, the long rod will help you keep a hooked fish out of cover, and whip it quickly.

Redfish anglers ask a lot from their tackle. In the coastal environment, gear is subjected to salt baths and the insidious creep of corrosion. Salty air alone encourages corrosion and stickiness in moving parts.

Rods and reels will get soaked, so they must be made corrosion-resistant, specifically for saltwater use. And, they must also be built strong enough to withstand wild boat rides. Crossing rough bays and venturing through dicey inlets, rods and reels may bounce in their holders and pound against gunnels and decks, potentially fracturing graphite, twisting guides and bending bails. One way or another, redfishing will expose the weaknesses caused by every grain of salt in a reel, every slight fracture of graphite in a favorite rod and every knick in a line.

Your tackle has to take a pounding, and come back for more. But your redfish tackle has to display a sensitive side, too. It must perform exceedingly well in the casting department. Extralong casts are often needed for spooky redfish, so you can't fish with a broomstick. You also usually have to cast accurately, at least when sight casting or working structure, so sensitivity is a factor both in casting and in feeling the take. And in terms of casting distance and sensitivity, reels and lines play an almost equally important role while pursuing redfish.

The drags in modern spinning reels are marvels that hold up to saltwater immersion and brutal runs.

Spinning Gear

Spinning tackle is often the most expedient choice in tackle. It excels on open water where the wind is blowing directly into your cast. In virtually any scenario, spinning outfits are the choice for making long, tangle-free casts. Spinning reels also retrieve line faster than most casting reels, which is very important when keeping up with slack fishing line and a hooked red.

Spinning Rods

Many quality spinning rods are built on high-modulus graphite blanks, which are strong, sensitive and light in weight. Rod companies also design rods around blanks

constructed with a combination of graphite and glass. By using special resins to bond the two materials, they provided added strength in a reasonably light rod.

Most spinning rods used for shallow-water reds are between seven and eight feet long. However, some companies offer 6- to 6½-foot rods with short butts for those who like to wade chest deep, and for working overhanging structure such as docks and mangroves. Most inshore redfish rods are designed to cast lures weighing from ¼ to 1¼ ounces, and are rated for 8- to 20-pound-test lines. Lure and line ratings are important, but flex, often identified as action, is the most important consideration.

A fast-action rod is very stiff. It has a stout butt section, which is ideal for fighting large redfish and making long casts. The middle third of the rod is also stiff, with the flexible section located in the upper quarter. There may be a little wobble in the tip, but not much.

Fast-action rods punch through strong winds, plus they offer a more direct connection to the lure. When fishing jigs in seagrass, they help pop the lure out of the grass and up through the water column with less chance of grass catching on the hook. They drive hooks through plastic and into bone and cartilage much more powerfully than "softer" rods.

Keeping a fish out of the mangroves, the author pushes a spinning rod to the flex max.

Sensitivity is another attribute. Finally, they're great for short-range work and for skip-casting under mangroves and docks. The added stiffness also helps you land more fish in such tough neighborhoods.

A medium-fast rod gets limber a little closer to the butt, in the upper third of the blank. Typically a medium-fast flex allows for longer casts with lighter baits and lures, because of the increased parabolic action. Both the weight of your lure and line bend the rod more deeply during the back cast, resulting in longer casts. If you're slinging Texas-rigged live shrimp or crabs at reds, go with a medium-fast rod. You'll also get a little more distance and softer landing when casting light plastic shrimp lures and small jerkbaits to reds in really skinny water.

Spinning Reels

Saltwater spinning reels have come a long way in recent years, partly because of the demands of anglers chasing redfish. Modern reels are constructed of super-light aluminum and graphite for increased strength and durability. Specially treated stainless steel ball bearings resist corrosion, while new synthetic drag washers last longer. Larger and longer reel spools and more stainless steel ball bearings promise improved line capacity, line management and casting distance.

GUIDE'S PICK SPIN
Capt. Mark Nichols

Rod
· 7-foot, 4-inch fast tip Shimano Calcutta

Reel
· 2500 Shimano Sustain

Line
· 15-pound Power Pro braid

Leader
· 20-pound Seaguar or Gamma fluorocarbon

Match your reel to your rod to ensure that the outfit has a balanced feel. There is no universal sizing of spinning reels; manufacturers assign various numbers and letters to their own products. You can start by selecting a line class

Fortunately, small-diameter braided lines have made it possible to use smaller, lighter reels without sacrificing line capacity.

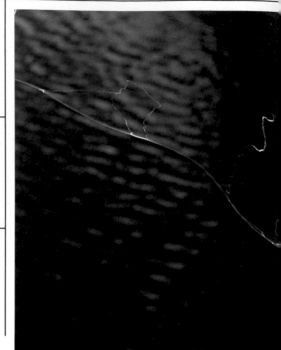

appropriate for the rod, and buying a reel that will hold an ample amount of that pound test. You need a minimum of 150 yards of line for inshore redfishing. But starting with 200 yards is advisable, since you will presumably break fish off, and hang up and get backlashes, all of which require cutting line and reducing the total amount.

Again, balance is paramount. You don't want a heavy rod with a petite reel, or worse, a light rod with a winch on it. For all-day casting, it's best to err on the light side. Fortunately, small-diameter braided lines have made it possible to use smaller, lighter reels, without sacrificing line capacity. These lines can give you three times the breaking strength relative to diameter that monofilament can. However, braided line has certain disadvantages in specific conditions, and reels that do not wind evenly cause nightmarish snarls in braid. So, you have to decide whether you intend to fish primarily with braided line or mono.

Generally speaking, an 8-pound-class spinning reel matches the short wading rods and your medium-fast-action rods. A 12-pound-class reel matches slightly heavier fast-action rods. And a 15- or 20-pound spinner goes on your bull red rod.

Multiple reels spooled with lines that are different materials, color and tests. Situations and lures call for specific lines.

Spinning reels are so named because during the cast, line spins off the reel in one direction and is spun back on by the rotor.

This angler used a relatively stout medium-heavy spinner to pull a red from jetty rocks.

Casting Gear

For both practical and traditional reasons, saltwater "baitcasting" or "plug casting" rods dominate the Texas market, and are preferred for specific applications everywhere. Most Texas anglers spend lots of time wading, and plug rods with short handles allow for longer casts and make imparting lure action easier when you're standing chest deep. Plug reels also tend to be more resistant to the elements than spinning gear. They have stronger drags, and you can thumb the reel easily to increase pressure on a fish. Finally, they're great for working shorelines because you can stop a flying lure on a dime simply by stopping the spool with your thumb.

Baitcasting Rods

Long-handled rods are great for search casting, as they allow for two-hand casting and maximum distance. Shorter-handled rods are best for a long day of making pinpoint casts with plugs, spoons and spinnerbaits to mangrove shorelines, grass edges and other structure.

Most plug-casting devotees use an under-

Shorter rods and handles make underhan

handed "roll cast" to land the lure in the red's strike zone without waving a fishing rod in its face like a red flag. A shorter rod with a shorter handle facilitates this style of fishing. Simply thumb the spool at the exact instant when the lure hovers over the bull's eye, and the lure drops on the spot.

Casting rods are also hard to beat in terms of hook-setting power, particularly when fishing with Texas-rigged lures or lures that employ large saltwater hooks or bait hooks. An angler first detects the strike, reels in the slack line, places the thumb on the spool and sets the hook firmly. This type of hookset, performed with a fast-action casting rod, almost always ensures a solid hookup.

Most plug casters take several rods. For mak-

Wading, *Florida Sportsman* editor Jeff Weakley and *Shallow Water Angler* regional editor Bobby Abruscato "hire" 7-foot baitcasters with softer tips for distance.

roll casting and punching shorelines easier.

ing long casts with lures weighing from ¼ to ¾ ounces, "hire" a 7-foot casting rod rated for 10- to 20-pound line. A fast-action rod with a medium-heavy butt is best for jigging, fishing suspending plugs and for weedless baits—applications that require a direct connection and quick and firm response. But elect a slightly softer rod for topwater "walking" plugs, spoons and spinnerbaits. You don't want to make much of a hookset using these lures; just reel down on the fish or you're liable to pull the lure away instead of letting it hook itself. Rods with a little more flex in the tip give excitable anglers some margin for error. Plus, they let you cast these heavy lures even farther.

Wading anglers prefer 6- to 6½-foot casting rods with shortened rear grips, so that the rod doesn't catch inside shirt sleeves or contact the water. Again, a medium-heavy butt section on a blank rated for 10- to 20-pound line is recommended. Lure weights would also remain the same as for the 7-foot casting rod, ranging from ¼ to ¾ ounces. Flex preference depends on lure type, but generally shorter casting rods are stiffer, or faster.

Baitcasting Reels

Like modern saltwater spinning reels, saltwater casting reels are also made of corrosion-resistant parts, including stainless steel bearings, aluminum or graphite frames and durable, synthetic drag washers.

There are two basic designs. The first is the standard round reel. Some top tournament anglers, such as *Shallow Water Angler* Central Gulf Regional Editor Bobby Abruscato, use round baitcasting reels exclusively, for everything. Others prefer the round reel when making long search casts, due to increased line capacity, and for bait fishing with heavier line, for the same reason.

The second is the low-profile reel, more lightweight and ergonomic. These reels fit in the palm of your hand.

Removable side plates allow fishermen to change spools with fresh line, or swap for a spare spool filled with a different diameter fish-

Gear-speed ratio is an important consideration.

Sturdy round reel, right, is the classic design. Low-profile reels, left, are lighter and easier on the hand. Inshore plug reels have level-winding mechanisms, a part which ensures that line is wound on evenly across the spool.

ing line. You have a choice of a side button or centered thumb bar for disengaging the spool for casting. With either style of reel, magnetic or centrifugal brakes applied to the revolving spool can be adjusted to minimize backlashing while making casts on a windy flat.

Plug reels come with various line retrieve ratios. If you're crawling soft plastics and jigs through grass, you may want a reel with a 4.5:1 or 5:1 ratio. These "low gear" reels also apply more torque on big fish headed for the bushes. Choose a reel with a 5.7:1, 6.2:1 or even 7:1 gear ratio for working spoons, topwater plugs and spinners.

Slower reels offer greater torque, but faster reels pick up line more quickly.

Plug rods have "triggers" which allow for a stronger grip and better lure action.

Fly Gear

F ly fishing for redfish is more akin to hunting, at least while sight fishing. You first stalk the fish, and then cast a small fly within a few feet of the fish's mouth. But if you have the wrists, shoulders and the will for it, blind casting flies along shorelines or even on open grassflats is very effective.

Fly Rods

Fly rods are rated by line weight, according to number. A 0-weight rod is used for 4-inch brook trout in the tiniest streams. A 15-weight is used for sailfish, tuna and other ocean giants. Seven- through 10-weight rods are

versatile. The medium-fast action 8- or 9-weight is capable of making very delicate presentations. Fast-action rods of the same weight can punch a small or medium-size fly through the wind, including poppers. And they can drag redfish out of spartina grass. The 10-weight is reserved for large streamers and poppers, or for bull reds.

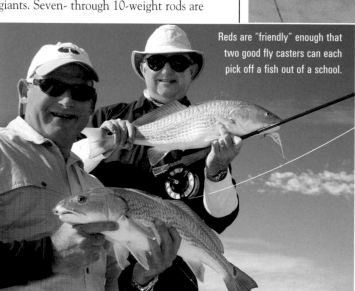

Reds are "friendly" enough that two good fly casters can each pick off a fish out of a school.

most commonly used in redfishing, and most rods sport either a medium-fast or fast action.

The 7-weight is reserved for casting small flies on calm days to spooky reds in clear, shallow water. Some days, especially in the winter months when most coastal waters are super-clear, a good fly caster can outfish experts using artificial lures and spinning or plug tackle. At times, the only thing these fish will eat is a tiny shrimp or crab imitation, presented at the end of a light, 9-foot fluorocarbon leader, without so much as a ripple.

Eight- and 9-weight rods are much more

As with spinning and casting rods, flex determines the character of a fly rod, even more so than line weight. In fact, the line weight assigned to the rod is more recommendation than rule. For example, an 8-weight, weight-forward floating line may not load a very stiff, fast-action rod that is marketed as an 8-weight. Such a rod may load much better with a 9-weight line. (Beginners will benefit from overloading their rod by one line weight, so that they can feel the rod load, or bend, more dramatically.) Conversely, some of the slower medium-action rods designed for casting larger loops with sinking lines can feel a little overburdened if you try to cast a tight loop with a floating or slow-sinking line with

the same number as the rod.

Most fly rods used in redfishing are in the 9-foot range. Some manufacturers make 9-foot, 6-inch and even 10-foot rods for wade fishing, but a 9-footer usually suffices. Like plug casters, anglers working overhanging structure such as docks and mangroves often prefer shorter sticks. An 8- or 8-foot, 6-inch 8- or 9-weight is better suited for "brush beating" and "dock darting."

The same amount of pressure is applied to two rods. The rod on the left is a slower action rod—better for sinking lines. The rod on the right has a fast action—perfect for on-the-money shots at tailing fish.

Fly Reels

Early fly reels didn't do much more than hold line. Modern reels are made from lightweight aluminum, and have features such as adjustable disc drags and quick-release spools for changing lines. Some also boast larger spools, or "arbors." All fly reels have a 1:1 gear ratio, and while large-arbor reels weigh a little more, they have an advantage in how quickly they pick up line. Because the revolution distance is greater a large-arbor reel picks up more line per turn than a reel with a standard arbor.

Large-arbor reels can feel a bit unwieldy on

Fly reels come in different sizes to match different line sizes. Some are "large arbor" reels, which increase the rate of retrieve.

7- and 8-weight rods. For most redfishing, a fly reel needs to hold at least 100 yards of 20-pound backing, and you can easily pack that much line and more on if you use 20-pound braided line on a standard size reel. All fly reels are marked for a specific line weight or for a narrow range of line weights. If you intend to overload your rod, you need to purchase one size larger reel, or cut down on the amount of backing so that the fly line isn't crammed too tightly on the reel.

Off to the races! A red's first burst is impressive in shallow water. Set your drag light and palm the spool.

Monofilament and
braided lines have
their respective
advantages. Braid
is best for casting
distance and sensi-
tivity. Mono flexes,
an advantage when
using topwaters.

Lines

In a simpler time, all anglers had to do was decide which pound-test monofilament to use. Today the plethora of monofilament, hybrid, fused and braided lines can be bewildering. But each type of line has its own set of advantages.

Monofilament

Monofilament is still one of the best, inexpensive and most versatile types of line available for redfishing. Monofilament is made by melting and mixing nylon and feeding the end product through tiny holes, forming the line, which is then spun into spools of various thicknesses. It can be used on spinning reels, spincasting reels, and baitcasting reels, or for fly leaders. Manufacturers can tweak the process to give mono color, improved knot strength, better abrasion resistance and other characteristics.

Mono stretches under pressure, which has advantages and disadvantages. Line stretch reduces your leverage as a fish exerts pressure on the other end; however, it also allows for some extra reaction time when a fish runs, and tighter drag setting. You don't get the sensitivity or hookset power that you do with spun braided lines, but many topwater enthusiasts prefer mono to braid, because it also floats high but is less likely to foul treble hooks. Some contend that the stretchiness of mono enhances the action with certain lures, such as crankbaits. Finally, if fly fishing with surface poppers or deerhair flies, remember that fluorocarbon sinks and will hinder the action or drown the deer hair. Make sure to use a monofilament leader when fishing on top with flies.

Hybrid lines

"Hybrid" lines are fairly recent innovations. These include nylon copolymer-resin monofilaments and nylon/fluorocarbon combinations. Like most monofilaments, these lines stretch under pressure, but may offer greater flexibility than ordinary mono. This allows for greater casting ease and accuracy. Line strength, diameter and price are typically on par with various high-quality monofilament, but with improved abrasion resistance. Fluorocarbon is made from an extruded polymer in a process similar to that of monofilament, but the composition of the material is said to be less visible under water, among other characteristics.

Braided Line

Braided lines are made by braiding or fusing fibers of gelspun polyethylene. One advantage of braid is the strength it offers relative to diameter. For example, 20-pound-test Fireline "braid" has the same diameter as 6-pound monofilament.

Braid is very fine, limp and does not stretch. So, it's super-sensitive—so sensitive you can feel a nibble with a hundred yards of line out,

Braids are made by braiding or weaving fibers of a synthetic material like Spectra or Micro-Dyneema into a strand of line.

or down. The tiny diameter plus the lack of memory and friction also allow for much longer casts. In terms of abrasion resistance, braid is orders of magnitude tougher than other types of fishing line. It is also very visible, and comes in a variety of dull and bright colors. For these reasons, it is popular among

Avoid "braid buggers." Wind the line tightly onto the spool.

redfishermen making long casts on the flats and working around structure.

There are significant cons to fishing with braid. Most significantly, it's two to three times as expensive as monofilament. It is also very visible in the water, so unless you're fishing very dark water you must tie on a monofilament or fluorocarbon leader. Joining lines made of two different materials has always been problematic because one material is inevitably a different diameter and finish and apt to slip through the knot. Braided line and fluorocarbon are vastly different materials, and making a strong connection is not easy. It requires an Albright knot, or a double uni-knot. Many anglers tie a double line in their lightest braid when tying to heavy mono or fluoro.

Unless you spool it exactly right, with appropriate tension and amount of line, so-called "braid knots" will make you pine for the relative simplicity of picking backlashes out of monofilament. If that knot gets wet, you'll never in a thousand years get the tangle out, so break out the scissors.

Some anglers also dislike braided line because it's so strong it can be hard to break when they get hung up. You can even break your rod because of the lack of stretch if you set the hook too hard. Plus, braided lines are coarse and minutely serrated and can make painful incisions into fingers. Some anglers like it because it floats and is therefore an advantage when fishing with topwaters. But because of the lack of stretch, there is the danger that may pull the bait away from a striking fish. You must set the drag softly enough that you don't rip the hooks out of its mouth if it makes a strong run. Finally, cutting braided line requires a very sharp pair of scissors. Clippers and pliers don't work very well.

Fly Lines

All fly reels used for redfishing should have about 200 yards of backing, and this material is usually either a gel-spun material, Dacron or Micron. The only downside of the lower-diameter braid is its tendency to cut things, such as the flyline at the loop connection, and you.

Flylines are woven synthetic strands coated with several thin layers of plastic. The weight and thickness of these coatings create three distinct types of lines: lines that float (floating), lines that sink gradually (slow- and intermediate-sink), and

From left, an intermediate-sink line, a fast-sink line, a floating line with a saltwater taper, and a floating line with an aggressive heavy head to penetrate wind.

lines that sink rapidly (sinking). The lines come in different sizes, shapes and weights for different casting situations. Most are numbered to match a weight of rod; for example, an 8-weight weight-forward line for an 8-weight rod. However, sinking lines are often described in terms of grains, or by some other numerical assignment that has to do with their weight or sink rate.

Weight-forward floating lines have a heavier "head" toward the front of the line. These are most commonly used in salt water. Slow- and intermediate-sink lines are useful for deeper flats and for schooling fish along beaches and shoals.

Heavy sinking lines are usually "shooting heads," very short, heavily weighted heads on the end of a "running line." Running lines are usually much thinner, plastic-coated lines. Some sinking lines are uniformly tapered or only slightly larger up front. The only redfish applications for heavy sinking lines are for targeting them in deep, fast-running inlets or passes, under pogy schools off the beaches, in heavy surf or on offshore live bottom.

Shallow Water Angler editor Mike Conner finds fly fishing in Carolina marshes a "kick in the grass."

Terminal Tackle

Leader size, as well as hook size and shape, vary tremendously from one style of redfishing to another. In shallow, clear water, a fly caster may go as small as a No. 4 fly and 12-pound fluorocarbon. But a surf caster may sling a baited 7/0 circle hook on 50-pound fluoro. "Bass"-style hooks are used frequently when fishing with soft-plastic baits. Knots vary from burly to sleek and slim.

Leaders

Terminal tackle involves leaders—the piece of line attached directly to the fly, lure or bait. Redfish usually live in structure-rich environments, and their lips, gill plates, tails and fins can abraid light lines. Many situations call for a shock leader between your fishing line and lure. This can be as light as 12- or 15-pound-test fluorocarbon, when fishing for spooky fish on shallow, clear flats, or as heavy as 50-pound-test when fishing for bull reds.

Usually, the shock leader is attached to the main line with a knot such as the double uni-knot, Albright special, blood knot or surgeon's knot. Occasionally, and usually when live or dead baiting with egg sinkers, a swivel makes the connection between the main line and the leader. The swivel should be larger than the diameter of the hole through the egg sinker, so it cannot slide down to the hook. Snap swivels are another type of hardware used to reduce line twist when fishing lures that spin, such as certain spoons.

When fishing the middle and lower portions of the water column, fluorocarbon is the best leader material because it has negative

buoyancy, is virtually invisible and is much more abrasion-resistant than monofilament. Use monofilament when fishing with topwater lures, since it floats and will not interfere with the lure's action.

Fly leaders are a different animal. Obviously you cannot attach a fly directly to the fly line. So, a butt section is attached to the fly line with a nail knot, Albright special, or is looped onto a served (whipped) loop at the end of the

Monofilament floats; fluorocarbon sinks. When fishing with topwater plugs or flies, use mono leaders. But subsurface, fluorocarbon has all the advantages.

fly line. The butt section should be monofilament, and of similar diameter to that of the end of the fly line. For 8- to 10-weight fly lines, 30- or 40-pound mono is perfect. A number of manufacturers sell pre-made fly leaders. Nine-foot monofilament leaders that taper down to 12- or 16-pound test are perfect for slot fish on relatively structure-free flats. You can add a short piece of fluorocarbon if you need a shock tippet or want the fly to sink more quickly.

Many fly anglers prefer to custom build tapered leaders for specific scenarios. When sight casting to tailing reds in the spartina grass, you don't want a long leader, or a light one. Six feet is plenty, and use fluorocarbon because the grass is sharp and you want the fly to sink. If you're throwing popping bugs or deerhair bugs, you want to use a slightly stiff monofilament, one that has the "guts" to turn over such a big fly.

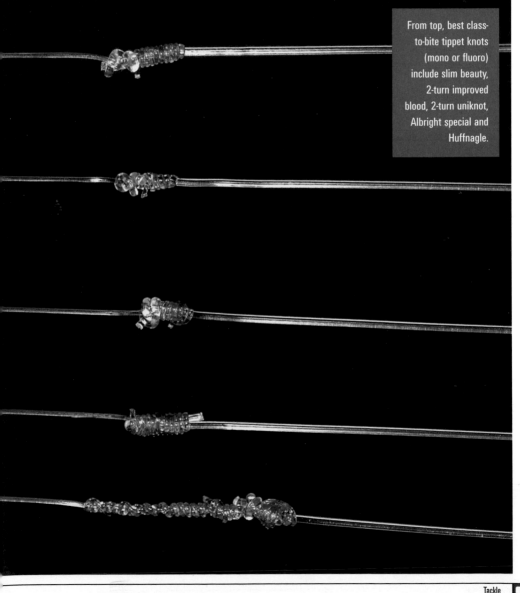

From top, best class-to-bite tippet knots (mono or fluoro) include slim beauty, 2-turn improved blood, 2-turn uniknot, Albright special and Huffnagle.

Bait Hooks

Hook selection depends almost entirely on your chosen technique, with a few general rules. Circle hooks have become increasingly popular among bait fishermen, as some authorities contend fish are more apt to swallow traditional J hooks, leading to unacceptable post-release mortality. It's rare to gut hook a redfish

Hooked through the tail, a shrimp can "flee" in reverse as it would naturally.

using circle hooks. Odds are the fish survive, if handled briefly and gently. Furthermore, it's rare to lose or miss a redfish using a circle hook, as the hook almost always finds its way into the corner of the mouth.

Hook size is a function of bait size. Use a No. 1 circle hook in a shrimp or small baitfish, such as a pilchard. A 5/0 or 6/0 circle hook fits a larger mullet or Atlantic menhaden, or a chunk of either bait.

Jerkbait Hooks

Jerkbaits can be rigged a variety of ways on thin wire offset hooks. Offset hook sizes for jerkbaits appropriate for redfishing run from 3/0 to 5/0, perhaps even 6/0. With jerkbaits, you can leave a little more tail free to undulate. Redfish tend to devour them, as they don't have any built-in hard or heavy parts. But always choose the larger gap when practical.

Heavy Live Bait Hooks
Good for larger finfish and cut baits.

Kahle-style Hooks
Good for threading live shrimp or for weedless jerkbaits.

Circle Hooks
Almost always stick in the corner of the mouth. Rarely swallowed, so the best bet for a successful catch and release.

Weighted Worm Hook
Here, there's no need to run the hook through the bait; "hitchhiker" screws into the jerkbait.

Worm Hooks
Excellent for rigging jerkbaits weedless.

Weedless "Tex-posed" jerkbait. The hookpoint rides right on top of the plastic.

Jigheads and Tails

Jigheads come in a variety of weights and hook lengths, but the hooks are almost uniformly steel J hooks. The most important consideration in hook length is the size of the soft plastic you intend to pin to it. You don't want the tail too far from the hook, or a redfish may short strike. The tail shouldn't be more than 1½ inches from the back of the hook.

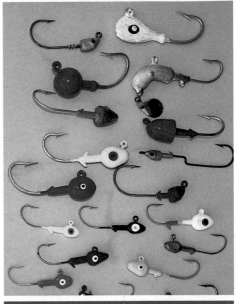

Left, an almost infinite variety of soft-plastic baits are matched with myriad shapes of jigheads, above.

Fly Hooks

Most flies are tied with a steel or thin-wire J-hook or J-hook variation. However, a few conservation-minded fly anglers tie flies onto circle hooks. They're effective, but it's difficult to break the habit of setting the hook forcibly on the strike, a no-no with circles. Hooks for popping bugs are unique. Mostly they are thin wire and very sharp.

Poppers and spoon flies should be in every redfish angler's fly box.

Clouser Minnows can be tied on a variety of J-hooks with differing shank lengths.

Landing Gear

Rubber-mesh nets are easier on fish and hooks don't foul in them.

Tackle needs don't end with the hook on the end of the line. Several products are designed to help you land a fish and release it without hurting the fish or yourself. These include landing nets, fish-holding grippers, gloves, towels and hook removers.

Landing Nets

Landing nets come in a number of shapes and sizes. Make sure the net has a sufficient diameter to land as big a redfish as you expect to find locally. Many have telescoping handles, which allow you to reach out to your catch and still stow it conveniently. Net mesh is usually nylon, but rubber-mesh nets are much more fish-friendly. Rubber is soft, and doesn't remove the essential coating of slime, which protects the fish against disease. Hooks are also removed from rubber nets far more easily.

Some conservation-minded folks say it's best not to net a fish you plan to release, but a net helps you get a fish under control. Unless you're taking the fish home for dinner, you might leave the netted fish in the water and remove the hook there. Besides the slime issues, when you remove a fish from the water, it experiences several times the amount gravity that it does under water. It's not good for their organs, plus they obviously can't breathe above water. If you want to get a picture with your fish, wet your hands and support the fish with your hand under its abdomen. Hanging a

If you plan to release it, it's best not to lift a fish out of the water with or without a net. Different story if it's going in the cooler.

Lip-gripping devices are useful to stabilize a fish while unhooking it. Make sure to support the fish under the belly.

fish by the gills, lips or jaw can do irreparable damage to feeding and breathing organs, and dislocate vertebrae.

Grippers

A wrestler knows that if you control the head, you control the body. But controlling a fish's head actually prevents a full-on WWF showdown on the water. You can lip a redfish like a bass, but you risk hooking yourself if you do. And there are tiny teeth in there, which can scratch you. Metal or plastic grippers put some distance between hook and hand. Simply place the prongs

around the tip of the fish's lower jawbone and release the trigger. The weight of the fish causes the prongs to shut even tighter, and a locking mechanism keeps prongs in the tightest position. Some models even have shock absorbers to dampen a fish's efforts to escape.

Some grippers are also scales, although it can be harmful to a fish that you plan to release to hang it by the jaws to weigh it. That doesn't mean you shouldn't ever weigh that

Measuring your Catch

If you're fishing a tournament, or plan to take home a fish, it's imperative that you know and conform to the size- and bag-limit regulations. The Florida Sportsman Communications Network offers rulers for most states that have the size limits of the most popular gamefish species printed on them. Adhesive "bumper sticker" style rulers stick on the deck of a boat.

Some states, Louisiana and Georgia for example, have very liberal bag limits. As of this writing, you can keep five reds in those states. Five large redfish would feed a small army, and it's a real shame to freezer-burn redfish fillets. Better to self-regulate and take home just what you need to feed the family fresh fish. SB

trophy. One way is to place the fish in a net and hook the grippers to the rim of the net. Weigh the fish in the net and then release it. Then weigh the net and subtract its weight from the first measurement.

Gloves

Gloves protect both the fish and angler. Wet gloves remove less fish slime, while they protect the angler from hook points, fin pokes and a number of nasty marine diseases such as flesh-eating bacteria. Limbs and even lives have been lost to *Vibrio vulnificus*, a bacteria that likes back bays. Guides on Florida's St. Lucie River complained of staph infections during 2005, when the U.S. Army Corps of Engineers pumped 300 billion gallons of nutrient-laden, algae-bloom covered runoff into North America's most biologically diverse estuary. And many outbreaks of both diseases have occurred in Texas waters over the years.

Thick gloves let you hold a red by the rough mouth. Fingerless gloves are more for sun protection. Dehookers spare the fingers.

Hook Removers

Most hook removers have a U-shaped end with a narrow gap. Some have a trigger and pulley system. The design is simple but ingenious, as you simply slide the end down the line, over the hook and then twist in the opposite direction. Sometimes you just have to break out the pliers, but hook removers provide a lot of torque in a really tight place. They're also a lot easier on the fish, rather than wedging a pair of pliers between the jaws. Always avoid touching the gills. Finally, hooks are much easier to remove if you mash down the barb or barbs. Barbs aren't needed if you keep a tight line. SB

Big fish really wear themselves
out and take longer to revive.
Below, when the **tail shakes in**
your hand, it's time to **let it go.**

Releasing Reds

Red drum are a tough fish, and the survival
ratio of released fish is high. But there are a
few techniques and products you can use to
improve that ratio. If you have a good livewell,
you can put the fish in it until it's recovered.
Products such as Rejuvenade help revitalize
fish even more quickly.

If you don't have a livewell, point the fish
into the current and move it from side to side,
but not backward, forcing oxygenated water
through the gills. Release the fish when it kicks
vigorously at your hand. If you are fishing in an
area that porpoises, sharks or barracudas fre-
quent, do not release a red in open water or
they may be killed. Complex cover such as mangrove roots or spartina grass protect reds from
larger predators while they recover. If there's
no such cover around, release the fish into
water that is too shallow for large predators to
enter, unless the water is super warm.

CHAPTER 5

Redfish Boats

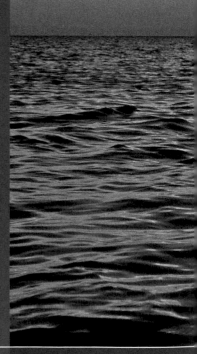

In recent years, we've seen exciting innovations in outboard engines and shallow-water fishing boats. Improvements in four-stroke and direct-injected two-stroke outboards brought better fuel efficiency and overall dependability.

Boat builders, too, have capitalized on lightweight composites and new resin technologies for a stronger, lighter craft. Canoes and kayaks have also evolved into custom-rigged flats fishing machines. Many redfish anglers own one or more boats, to fish different waters in different ways.

Technical poling skiffs are super-light boats designed for sight fishing in a few inches of water. Flats skiffs, the slightly larger and more comfortable varieties, can be poled across flats less than a foot deep. Crossover skiffs, large poleable flats skiffs in the 20- to 24-foot range, handle rough water much better than poling skiffs and accommodate up to four anglers. But they draw more water and aren't as easy to pole. Bay boats, though they may draw a foot of water or more, are perhaps the most comfortable inshore ride, and are often preferred where anglers must run across large, rough waterways. Finally, "car toppers," canoes and kayaks are loved for their portability and their ability to silently access the skinniest waters.

In many places, redfish are accessible via kayak, canoe, john boat, flats skiff and bay boat. Every boat is a compromise, but very specialized redfish boats are available.

See DVD for more on getting skinny.

Top, fly casting to reds from a poling skiff is a classic way to fish. Right, the sit-on-top kayak has become a favorite vessel for stalking old spot tail.

Poling Skiffs

Many serious redfishermen own two or more motor boats, one for fishing the bays and one for navigating the flats. The boat most commonly used for fishing the shallow flats is a poling skiff. These vessels range from about 15 to 19 feet, draw 5 to 10 inches of water and weigh as little as 500 pounds. The shallowest draft skiffs, sometimes called "technical poling skiffs," are 17 feet or less, are made of lightweight materials such as Kevlar and often have lightweight one-piece hulls. Max horsepower on these amazing little boats ranges from 25 to 70 hp, and many anglers opt for a tiller control to eliminate the need (and the weight) of a console. For those addicted to sight fishing on the shallowest flats, these are the ultimate rigs. Much study has also gone into making technical skiffs as stealthy as possible. Manufacturers talk about "hull slap," the sound of water striking

Top, sleek and fast, skiffs get you to the flat quickly, then go into stealth mode. Below, notice that both captains have the outboard skeg in the water to help track straight.

See DVD for more on poling the shorelines, see natural structure.

the bow as you pole, like it's a disease. So, chine systems are designed to divert spray created by a boat hull and to reduce noise.

You can't beat a good technical poling skiff in terms of shallow draft, stealth and poling ease, but you better buy a good foul-weather suit to go with your boat if you plan on running across big water. Slightly larger flats skiffs may not run or pole in extreme shallows, but they are more comfortable on open bays. Averaging 17 to 19 feet, these boats are a step up in length, weight and power from technical poling skiffs. Typically, these boats are somewhat heavier, roughly 700- to 1,400-pound hulls, and constructed to handle larger fuel cells, larger motors, more storage and likely have livewells. The fuel cell is normally a 30- to 50-gallon unit

installed in the middle of the hull, for balance. Maximum hp ratings normally range from 90 to 200. These larger flats boats are an excellent choice if you enjoy bay fishing but also wish occasionally to pole a fairly shallow flat.

Slipper Skiffs

Some of these glass slipper skiffs have V hulls, but the tunnel-hulled models are gaining favor. These boats typically sport a semi-circular concavity, or tunnel, on the centerline on the bottom of the hull. With other boats, the outboard's cavitation plate must be at least even or below the bottom of the boat. The tunnel allows the motor to be raised for shallow-water running; the tunnel channels cooling water to pickups on the lower unit, and enough water to give the prop a purchase even though it is above the boat bottom. It's a clever modification, opening up waters which may otherwise be hard to reach.

In the wrong hands any shallow-water skiff can become seagrass lawn mowers. But if you trim the engine correctly and run in realistic depths, the seagrass is safe. SB

Bay Boats

Bay boats were voted the most popular vessel type for redfishing, according to a survey of professional anglers on the Oboy! O'Berto Redfish Cup tournament series. The series includes many coastal waters including Texas bays, Louisiana bayous and Florida flats.

Bay boats range in length from 19 to 24 feet and can weigh up to 2,500 pounds. With their wide beams—up to 96 inches—and semi deep-V bottoms, bay boats float in fairly shallow water. Some bay boat manufacturers claim that their bay boats can float in as little as 10 inches. However, most will float from 12 to 15 inches, fully loaded.

Bay boats offer a dryer and softer ride than shallow-water skiffs, and more speed too, with sufficient power. Space-age stringer systems tie into the hull, transom and the deck to work as one unit. The result is less torque, where hull separation often takes place in boats that do not use a superior stringer system. Top of the line bay boats also use premium resins and hand-laid fiberglass components. Some brands integrate flotation compartments into their hulls to ensure an unsinkable boat.

While bay boats are often slightly heavier and use a little more fuel, large fuel cells give them impressive range. Most are rigged with a 70-gallon fuel cell, which may offer up to a 300-mile fishing range. Some bay boats can be rigged with up to 300 horsepower and are capable of 70 knots. Often, there's a leaning post and/or rocket launcher behind the center console command center.

Bay boats offer more freeboard and stability, making it easier to fish in open waters.

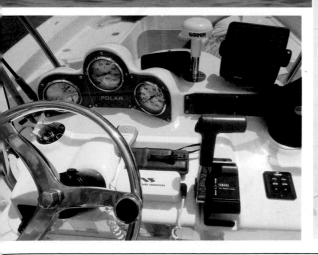

Bay boats allow three to fish comfortably. Tall center console allows driver to stand and accommodates gauges and gadgets. Below decks you find voluminous storage and livewells.

Crossovers

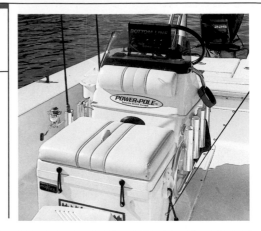

Nineteen- to 23-foot flats skiffs are sometimes called "crossover skiffs," mostly because they have small-skiff features, yet push the envelope size-wise, in terms of poling. You are much more likely to fish an area under trolling motor power than under shoulder power. But like smaller flats skiffs, crossovers usually have large flat areas on the bow to cast from, stern platforms, a pol-

Crossover skiffs aren't as easy to pole as a smaller skiff, but they take the pounding out of a long run. They have low center consoles and gunnels and more deck room for fishing than many bay boats, which have deeper cockpits.

ing platform and wide gunnels. Like bay boats, many of these larger skiffs have sharper hull entries, to project spray away from the boat. They also have more freeboard and weight, which allow the boat to part choppy waves.

In terms of fishing features, crossover skiffs provide much more room for amenities. These skiffs may have as many as two large livewells plus a release well. They have large compartments forward and aft capable of stowing multiple castnets and reams of tackle. Some even have lockable rod storage forward, as well as under-gunnel storage.

In short, crossover skiffs are great for the family angler who still wants to fish in a foot or two of water. They're also great for tournament anglers and anyone making long runs across open water to find fish.

The joke goes that you could hold a dance on the deck of a crossover skiff.

Flat-decked tunnel skiffs make landing and releasing fish easy

Texas Tunnels Sans Gunnels

Decades ago, Texas anglers developed a special catamaran hull capable of running in only a few inches of water.

A high, flared bow funnels air back through the tunnel, giving the boat lift. This unique design not only allows a catamaran bay boat to run in four inches of water, but also allows the boat to jump up on plane in 6 inches of water or less. Even large cat hulls, such as the 21-foot models weighing 1,400 pounds, run in about six inches.

Deadrise helps make a tunnel hull ride drier.

Tunnel skiffs with low gunnels, or no gunnels, and flat decks are immensely popular in Texas because most Texans wade or drift fish in very shallow water. The low gunnels make climbing into and out of the boat, and landing fish, easy. And most of the time, they're running great expanses of water that are just a foot or two deep for miles and miles. The chances of falling off and drowning are minimal, and it's rarely rough enough to make the spray a nuisance. "Scooter boats" are beloved by Texans, but they're catching on in other places where wade and drift fishing in calm expanses is popular.

Some manufactuers are building boats with higher gunnels for safety and comfort. Tall center consoles on scooter boats allow the driver to hide from spray and give room for storage.

Cartoppers

Canoes and kayaks rank among the most versatile, stealthy and certainly the most portable vessels. Going fishing is as easy as finding roadside access to an estuary, taking your boat off the roof, loading it and setting off.

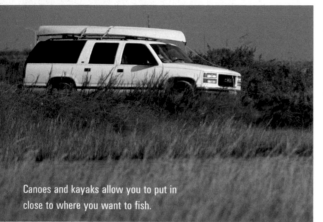

Canoes and kayaks allow you to put in close to where you want to fish.

Paddling is a great way to get some exercise and enjoy the serenity while fishing.

Your range is limited only by your strength, or by your capacity to carry provisions and willingness to camp. Kayaks have the advantage in terms of affordability, speed and stealth, but canoes are more stable, allow for "team" fishing and carry more gear.

Canoes

Most canoes used for saltwater fishing are 16 feet or longer, and fairly beamy. The top-end models are made of a carbon-Kevlar composite. They're super light, gorgeous and handle incredibly well. However, anglers fishing around oyster bars and other submerged structure may want to consider an aluminum or Duratex-finished boat. If your canoe will lead a hard life, go with these more durable materials.

A pair of athletic anglers can sight fish while standing in a stable canoe if they're careful. Anglers who have trouble standing in the proverbial "tippy canoe" can fasten outrigger pontoon stabilizers to gunnels, such as the

popular snap-in floats by Spring Creek outfitters. Outriggers dip in the water while you pole, and thus are a liability in terms of stealth. But they sure are convenient if you're using the canoe to carry you into position to wade. Getting in and out of the boat is much less of a mission.

Manufacturers discuss canoe stability in terms of "primary" and "secondary" stability. Primary stability refers to the boat's relative stability when it is not moving; secondary stability refers to the boat's stability while under way. Of course, primary stability is very important for saltwater fishing and the degree of stability is largely a function of bottom configuration.

Flat-bottomed boats provide the most room for gear and are stable to a point, but there's a distinct point of no return once the boat tips past the chine. You lose contact with the wetted flat surface that stabilizes the canoe. They're also slow to accelerate and sluggish through turns. Better to buy what's called a shallow-arched or shallow-rounded hull. The arches or rounds, V-entry and keel combine functions to provide resistance as the boat tilts.

Rocker, the curvature of the keel line, is another important performance factor. Boats with almost two inches of rocker or more will be very agile, but squirrelly for fishing. One and one-half to 1¾ inches of rocker is in the good compromise range for anglers who work bays and lakes, but also fish in creeks and rivers. If you fish more frequently in swift-moving tidal creeks, you may want to go with a little more rocker. But if you fish open water mostly, and especially in cold, open water, you really need a sharp keel for tracking straight, cutting through chop and allowing you to enjoy the glide.

Kayaks

Kayak fishing is growing in popularity. For example, 282 kayaking anglers entered the 2007 Jacksonville Florida Kayak Fishing Classic. It's no fad; kayaks are deadly fishing machines. Hull slap is a non-issue—you can get so close to tailing redfish you can touch tail with the end of your rod, even in the shallowest

See DVD getting skinny for more on paddling for reds.

Stabilizers allow anglers to stand in a big canoe to pole and fight fish.

Left, canoe/kayak hybrid with stabilizers and drift sock allow an angler to drift fish while standing. Below, angler uses a spike anchor to hold position during the fight.

water. Lightweight, polyethylene materials allow a kayak to float in two to three inches.

Most saltwater anglers prefer the sit-on-top variety because you can get out of the boat to wade more easily. They're better at navigating rough water than canoes.

As with canoes, the longer the boat the faster it is. Long, narrow boats are called "touring boats," and they fly. Dedicated touring boats are sit-inside models, and only the angler interested in long-range kayak-fishing adventures needs to consider touring boats, which are generally 13 to 18 feet, with a beam of less than 28 inches.

Most kayaks built with fishing in mind are 9 to 13 feet, with beams from 28 to 34 inches. The wider the kayak the more stable the boat, and an athletic angler can easily stand in the wider models to fish. (As with canoes, a number of companies also make outrigger pontoons for added stability.) Short models and models made for women and kids weigh as little as 35 pounds, and carbon/Kevlar models are as light as 18 pounds. But your average 13-foot, sit-on-tip kayak ranges from 50 to 70 pounds.

Kayaking is great exercise for the shoulders, arms, back and stabilizer muscles; that is if you're using a paddle. Pedal power is an old technology but relatively new in terms of fishing use. Foot pedals drive penguin-like flippers to propel the craft. Although almost twice the price, pedal boats are faster and quieter. Most importantly, they leave hands free to fish. But, they don't operate in as shallow water.

Storage capacities and fishing options vary widely brand to brand and model to model. Storage accessibility also varies widely from kayak to kayak. Where space comes at a premium, hatch-lid designs range from nightmarish to ingenious simplicity. Some even allow fully rigged fly rods to be stowed inside. SB

Kayak Options Aplenty

Kayaks can be custom-rigged for redfishing. Customizations include rod and net holders, shade devices, GPS units and stabilizers. Make sure to put one rod holder behind the seat in vertically or tilted toward the stern for trolling while paddling.

More than a John—Aluminum Skiffs

Aluminum boats are less expensive , take a beating and are easy to repair.

John boats rigged with a small outboard are affordable, effective vessels used in many areas. Aluminum boats are a great choice when fishing oyster bars, since you can bang up against and drag over sharp oysters with minimal damage to the hull.

You can custom rig your aluminum boat with a poling platform and casting deck at the bow. A 72-quart cooler, plumbed with a recirculating pump can act as a livewell.

The major fishing drawback with an aluminum boat is hull noise and minimal storage for fishing rods and gear. Small portable or small factory-installed fuel cells can also be a limiting factor in terms of range. Flat-bottom aluminum boats will dole out a pounding in rough water.

Some anglers who stalk skinny water only part of the time, or fish or duck hunt in areas where combustion engines aren't allowed, opt for canoe/skiff hybrids. The classic Gheenoe is a 16-foot, square-back canoe with a whopping 4 feet, 7 inches of beam. Some anglers build poling platforms toward the stern, and add stabilizers. East Cape canoes are another popular and affordable, but more skiff-like large canoe.

Aluminum skiffs need more customizing than most boats. Customizations may include bow seat, top, rod racks, middle, and poling platform, right.

Gheenoe with Go-Devil, pushpole and electric motor. Pick your propulsion.

CHAPTER 6

Rigging Your Redfish Boat

Kayaks, canoes and a variety of skiffs and bay boats make up the shallow-water redfish fleet. Boats should be customized for the styles of fishing you do most. Jack plates allow for super-shallow running. Trim tabs keep the boat at an optimal attitude. Poling platforms are de rigueur on flats skiffs, and some bay boat owners like a perch, too. Bow-mounted casting platforms offer a serious advantage for sight fishing. Some stealth-conscious anglers install non-skid marine traction on the decks and in the cockpit, which also reduces foot, leg and back fatigue. Livewells keep bait or reds frisky. Vertical rodholders keep sticks handy; rod lockers keep them down and out of the way when fly casting. Choosing the right options will lend considerably to your fishing success.

Redfish boats are sleek, fast and stealthy. They're going places where no boat has gone before.

Proper trim is evident by the evenness of the wake. Having the engine tilt and trim tabs working together helps the boat hold through tight turns at high speeds.

This technical poling skiff, complete with trim tabs, Power-Pole, platform and trolling motor, is a tribute to form and function. It's enough to make a gondola skipper green with envy.

Tricked Out for Success

An angler's platform is his or her castle. Keep the ergonomics of poling and fishing from the platform in mind while customizing.

L adies know; it's all about accessorizing. That includes redfishing. No matter what boat or boats you buy, including flats skiffs, bay boats and cartoppers, there are essential accessories to help you pursue redfish. These include poling platforms, pushpoles, bait- and release wells, anchoring systems, leaning posts, electric motors and a suite of appliances for canoes and kayaks.

Poling Platforms

During the pioneer days of flats fishing, the captain poled the boat backwards, from the bow, while standing on the deck. As skiffs evolved, captains began poling from the stern, but still from the deck. Towers and elevated command stations already existed, but a little over 40 years ago, Miami, Florida, flats-fishing pioneer Capt. Bill Curtis invented the first poling platform designed specifically for sight fishing on the flats.

Poling platforms give anglers multiple advantages, whether sight fishing or not, but the primary advantages facilitate the most exciting way to fish—team sight fishing. The platforms come in several different sizes and widths, with the lower and smaller ones reserved for technical poling skiffs and squareback canoes. Most offer a 3- to 4-foot elevated platform that affords the poling angler a high perch to spot fish. Or, if you're under electric motor power, one angler can get the bird's eye view by fishing from the platform. By standing higher, you can put the sun more or less behind you, and allow it to illuminate the flat instead of casting a veil of glare across it. Plus, a platform also gives the poler much more leverage, making poling into the wind and/or tide much less exercise.

Poling platforms are installed at the transom of the boat and over the outboard motor. They can be installed on any style of redfish boat, even bay boats. However, a heavier boat with a deep draft is harder to propel and to keep on course. The supports are often made from aluminum, with a side frame ladder and a fiberglass deck. Rod holders can be attached to the aluminum frame to store fishing rods for easy access when a school of redfish is "bumped," or for other fishing purposes such as trolling or trailing a live bait behind the boat.

Bungee strap holds pushpole while drifting or staked out. Stern light flips down and out of the way.

One of the greatest advantages in poling is the ability to anchor or "stake out" almost instantly, as when a school of reds is bearing down on you. In staking out, the pointed end of the pushpole is forced into the bottom at an angle and the opposite end of the pole is secured to the boat's poling platform with a cord, rope or clip. "Snubbers" are one option. These are concave rubber clips installed on the top of the platform. They are quiet and very easy to access. However, you can step and trip on them. Belt clips and clips that go on the side of the platform are also options. Some

Metal tips help prevent slippage over rock or shell bottoms while poling. The foot, below, is used in soft bottom. A clip holds the pole when staked out to make a cast.

anglers use Bungee cords which hook through an I-ring on the rubber foot of the pole. And there's always the old-fashioned way, a simple piece of rope looped around the pole and fastened to the supports with a knot.

Push Poles

Pushpoles range from the simple to the sophisticated, from a 12-foot PVC pipe with caps on the ends, to a graphite 20-foot leverage machine. Good pushpoles are lightweight and stiff with just enough flex to avoid breakage.

One end of the pushpole is pointed and used for staking out the boat and when poling on a hard bottom. The forked end is used for poling on a soft bottom. In Louisiana and other shallow-water environs with liquid-soft mud bottoms, anglers attach an even larger "mud shoe" so that the pole will not simply sink impotently into the bottom.

Most poles are fiberglass or graphite, or a combination of the two. Single-piece graphite poles are incredibly light. Twenty-foot models weigh as little as four pounds. But, they're expensive and will snap if, for instance, the pole gets stuck in a hole or in the mud and the wind and tide put too extreme a bend

in it. Fiberglass and graphite/fiberglass composites are stronger, and heavier. Some manufacturers do make graphite, two-piece poles. However, these are the most fragile pushpoles on the market because two-piece poles are inherently weaker than one-piece poles. If you want a two-piece pole so you can stow it under the gunnels, better to choose a model that is at least part fiberglass. There are shorter poles for kayaks and canoes that range from five to 14 feet.

Towers

In Texas bays and along Florida's Gulf coast, shallow-water anglers have taken a cue from the bluewater crowd and installed towers on larger skiffs and bay boats. Console towers can raise fishermen five or six feet above the deck for a real bird's eye view of flats. Console tow-

Towers are an option for bay boats and allow anglers to spot fish.

ers are normally hinged so they can be folded down for trailering. These may have full controls, including steering and throttle and even electronics. One caution about towers—they can be very dangerous. They make a boat top heavy, and fishermen have been seriously injured when tower boats have rolled over because of a large boat wake, ground swell or rough bay conditions.

Shallow Water Anchoring

Healthy grassflats are critical for redfish and almost every other inshore and reef-dwelling species of fish at some life stage. Traditional anchors can damage the grassbeds and bottom. Some conscientious anglers refrain from using a regular Danforth or mushroom-style anchor. Plus, they're noisy to deploy.

Staking out with your pushpole is a quiet and environmentally friendly way to anchor up. Another option is a 12-volt system called the Power-Pole, which sets a long, hydraulically operated composite spike into the bottom, at the push of a button on remote control keypad. The Power-Pole anchors a boat instantly without disrupting the bottom and is retrieved in the same manner.

The only problem with staking out with a pushpole or Power-Pole is that the wind and tide may swing the bow out of position. Along with a pushpole or Power-Pole, many anglers carry a Cajun Anchor, or another variety of "spear anchor." The Cajun Anchor was designed to hold in Louisiana mud. It's very quiet and deploys easily and is especially handy for kayak or canoe fishing. Fasten a rope to the I-ring, stick it in the bottom and tie off the rope on a forward cleat. The bonus is that when you are ready to pull anchor you can simply back off with your boat, which also cleans the device.

For canoes and kayaks and even small skiffs, bell anchors are the way to go.

Sea Anchors

Sea anchors or "drift socks" are chutes made of nylon, canvas or other sturdy material that you deploy to slow your drift over a flat. For anglers blind casting windy flats, such as those in Texas' Lower Laguna Madre, these devices are a must. One or more sea anchors can also be attached to boat cleats and used to slow the drift of your redfish boat. Secure the drift sock from the stern and the boat will drift more or

Casting Platforms

Just a foot or so of elevation helps casters see beyond the glare.

In the early days, captains carried stepladders so that anglers could get a better view of the flat. Some still do. More secure is a smaller version of the poling platform. "Casting platforms" can be installed at the bow of your redfish boat to give the angler some height advantage. These are usually about a foot to 18 inches in height and a little larger than home plate. The small raised deck doesn't take up all of your deck room on the bow. Generally, they're removeable, and secured to the deck with a turnbuckle, which is attached to the underside of the platform and to the deck.

Invest in a drift sock if you spend much time drifting in windy places. They don't cost much, and turn frustrating conditions into manageable ones.

less bow first downwind. Secure a drift sock from the side and the boat will "crab" across the flat sideways. You can also turn your outboard to influence direction and angle, and/or use an electric motor.

Livewells

Most shallow-water vessels come with one or multiple re-circulating livewells large enough to keep shrimp, crabs and larger baitfish alive for the trip duration. Some smaller boats, such as john boats or canoe/skiff hybrids may not have livewells, and of course canoes and kayaks don't come with them.

If fishing with shrimp or crabs, a small bucket with battery-powered aerator suffices. Since dragging a perforated bait bucket really slows you down, such systems are about mandatory in a canoe or kayak. Portable livewells are also available, with portable re-circulating pumps. In a motor boat, you will need to fasten the

Livewells keep baits frisky. Release wells, above, allow tournament anglers to carry fish alive back to the weigh station. They're also great for reviving exhausted fish before the release.

hoses to the stern or gunnel while running. Most canoes have sufficient room for a 10-gallon well amidships, and kayakers often fasten them behind the seat.

Boats rigged for tournament fishing also have 30-gallon or larger release wells, dubbed "fish hospitals." Release wells are typically very large and rectangular to accommodate redfish measuring in the upper slot. The best release wells have oxygen infusion systems; the O2 is supplied by a cylinder or 12-volt pump. Special additives such as Rejuvenade can be added to the water in the release well to help revive a fish.

Electric Motors

A bow-mounted electric motor is an excellent tool to guide your boat within poling distance of a school of redfish, or to navigate your boat within casting distance of redfish when they aren't spooked by electric motors. Modern electric motors are quieter than ever, due in part to the demands of redfishermen.

The key to successfully operating an electric motor on a shallow redfish flat and without spooking the school, is to operate the electric motor on low speed. Frequently changing the speed from low to high will spook shallow-water redfish. Also make sure that the electric motor propeller is not making contact with the bottom. This will not only damage the habitat and your propeller, but it will also spook nearby redfish.

When selecting an electric motor, make sure that the length of the shaft is long enough so that the propeller is completely in the water and not cavitating. Shaft sizes normally range from 50 to 60 inches. Bay boats and cats normally require the longer shaft, and more torque.

Electric motors also come in 12-, 24- and 36-volt models. Twelve-volt electric motors

Engine-mounted electric motors work best for chasing pods of fish in open and deeper waters. Top, bow-mounted electric allow you to work more slowly and in shallower water.

will work fine on an aluminum boat or small skiff and supply up to 54 pounds of thrust. Twenty-four volt electric motors work best on flats boats and offer 70 to 82 pounds of thrust. Thirty-six volt motors produce more than 100 pounds of thrust and work best on heavier bay boats.

Manufacturers also offer quick disconnect mounts that allow you to take the electric motor off the bow of your boat when you're only going to pole the boat, and you don't want the weight, or anything to catch fly line. A second mount can be installed on the rear deck so that the electric motor can be mounted from the rear deck when navigating rough bays. And custom electric motors can also be installed on your boat's trim tabs, or on your lower unit.

An onboard battery charger eliminates the need to charge each individual battery with a portable battery charger, but make sure it is made for saltwater use. These chargers can charge multiple batteries at one time, by simply plugging in a 110-volt extension cord.

The most recent models of trolling motors are controlled remotely, which frees the angler to move about the boat.

Anglers choose between three styles of electric motors, foot control, remote control and hand control. Hand control units are most dependable, and few saltwater anglers rely on foot pedals for corrosion reasons. Remote control technology has dramatically improved, and allows you to control your heading from anywhere in the boat. They really come in handy when you're trying to release a fish or re-rig.

Finally, make sure that you carry spare fuses on the water for your electric motor. And always unplug the power cord when the motor is not in use. SB

Electronics

Fishing electronics have improved dramatically, and these days even canoeists and kayakers rig GPS systems and other devices on their vessels. Many units are available today with Global Positioning Systems and bottom sounding capacities.

The "chart chip" is one of the best inventions. Boaters can purchase electronic charts that the machine uploads for virtually any inshore area in the country. When combined with crisp satellite photos of specific areas, these charts are the easiest way to learn a new area. Recently, Fugawi introduced a Google Earth plug-in that

You can now combine satellite imagery with highly detailed electronic charts.

allows you to view location imagery alongside the chart as you run.

By entering a waypoint, the GPS will help you navigate precisely to where you want to fish. Or, you can simply move the cursor to your destina-

tion and it will give you direction to steer and distance. A trail indicates where you you've been, and marks the way back home.

Units can also give you valuable information, including where oyster bars and wellheads are located. They also read depth and water temperature. Tides can also be shown by simply moving the cursor to a tide station icon on the map mode.

Fishfinders can also identify deep-water redfish habitat—scattered jetty rocks on the bottom, a deep slough on a flat, or deep and shallow portions of a marsh creek.

Finally, marine radios are a must to monitor local VHF channels. Your cell phone can't tell you where the fish are. But more importantly, you have a way to signal help if in distress and to monitor for other boats in dire straits. Hand-held units usually suffice inshore, but keep in mind that they have a more limited range than built-in units if you are fishing deep in wilderness.

GPS/fishfinder systems can be flush mounted in the console alongside a marine radio and gauges, or mounted on top.

CHAPTER 7

Tides

On most waters, tides are the primary external influence on redfish behavior. Tides determine whether redfish will feed on a flat or just off it, whether they'll sit in a hole in a pass or inlet, or just inside, or outside. The tide determines whether fish cruise through mangrove roots or along the first trough outside them, on an oyster bar or in nearby deep water. Current is one of the primary influences that trigger feeding.

With the exception of waters where tide isn't a factor, such as Florida's Banana River and southern Mosquito Lagoon, learning the tides is essential to becoming a good inshore angler. Some hard lessons, including 6-hour waits aground on a flat, may go with the territory. But that's part of the adventure.

Dozens of factors influence tides, especially wind. A strong wind blowing in the direction of an outgoing tide can leave a flat high and dry much earlier than predicted.

See DVD for more on your "window of opportunity."

Four hours after this photograph was taken, this maze of oyster bars on Northeast Florida's Amelia River was almost entirely under water. Throughout this region, tides range as much as 7 feet.

Tides 101

Redfish occur in both the Gulf and Atlantic basins. Tides are the result of the combined influences of the gravitational attraction of the moon and sun on the earth's seas. The local range and timing of

Reds will enjoy a crab lunch as soon as the tide floods the marsh.

water level changes will depend, to a large extent, on the shape or size of the basin, as well as its undersea and shallow contours. Tides generally move around the globe from east to west as the earth turns on its polar axis. Flood tides can be imagined as the crest of a wave circling the earth. In reality it's a bit more complicated that that.

The U.S. Atlantic coast has an orderly pattern of semidiurnal tides, meaning that there are two high tides and two low tides each day. However, tides are much more dramatic from Northeast Florida to southern North Carolina. The best fishing for reds in the flooding marsh

grass occurs during 6- to 8-foot tides.

On the Gulf of Mexico, along Florida's Panhandle and the Alabama, Mississippi, Louisiana and Texas coasts, predictable diurnal tides occur, with one high tide and one low tide daily. The fluctuations usually aren't more than two feet, and much less in Texas' Lower Laguna Madre. For example, the Mississippi River's Southeast Pass has very minor tidal fluctuations, which are partially offset by the river's flow. On April 1, 2007 a low tide occurred at 4:06 a.m. with a tide height of 0.7 feet, and at 9:37 a.m. a high tide produced a tide height of 1.7 feet.

"Ideally you have a falling tide all day," says Dauphin Island, Alabama Capt. Bobby Abruscato about fishing the Central Gulf coast. "As the water falls out of the marsh, the grass filters the water and clears it up enough to sight fish."

The Florida peninsula lies between two different basins, the huge, deep Atlantic and the relatively small Gulf of Mexico. These two basins respond differently to the tidal pull circling the globe. Because the southwest Florida coast is located right between these two distinct patterns, it has mixed tides: sometimes two high tides each day, sometimes one daily high tide, and sometimes an odd mixture of the two.

In some waters, such as Florida's Mosquito Lagoon, the Banana River and the upper Indian River Lagoon, there are no tides. Here water levels are mainly determined by precipitation and wind direction.

Dozens of factors influence tides, especially wind. A strong wind blowing in the direction of the outgoing tide can leave a flat high and dry much earlier in the ebb than usual.

Outflow from rivers, creeks and marshes lends to a greater tidal exchange. An excellent example is Texas' Sabine Pass and Galveston Bay. Here the tidal range averages about two feet. Myriad factors come into play, however. There are very few rivers flowing into the hypersaline Lower Laguna Madre, so the tide range averages only a foot or so.

A tide watch and tide charts are handy, but semidiurnal tide times are 50 minutes later each day, corresponding to moon rise 50 minutes later each day. The National Ocean Service reports times and heights of tides. Visit www.opsd.nos.noaa.gov and click on "Tide Predictions."

Often the slower moving phases of tides offer the best fishing. The first of the falling tide is a time to keep your lure in the water. It forces many of the redfish's favorite forage foods from their high-tide hideouts, making them easy prey.

Moon Phases

Full and new moon phases bring spring tides, the highest and lowest tides of the month, and the equinox tides are the year's most dramatic. Both low and high tide can be magnified by prevailing, strong winds. If high winds are blowing in from the Gulf or Atlantic Ocean, a full moon spring tide will flood areas of the marshes or bay that are generally high and dry. Redfish take advantage of these extreme tides and move farther back into the shallows to reach otherwise inaccessible prey.

In most regions full and new moons produce hard-running tides, which can also produce poor redfishing conditions in passes and inlets, because the current is too strong to anchor safely or keep baits and lures in the zone.

When booking a guided trip, or simply planning a day of redfishing, avoid fishing a few days following a full or new moon. During extreme high tides, redfish will take advantage during the first few days of the full and new moons to feed in rarely flooded habitats. After satisfying their appetites, they often develop a case of lockjaw for the next few days.

The best redfishing often comes during a week before a full moon and a week preceding a new moon. If you just have to target redfish during the full and new moon phases, fish the last few hours before dead low tide and the first few hours of the incoming tide. Or better yet, put on your wading shoes and wade the super flood tides for tailing redfish.

Full moon tides are the month's most extreme. These tides make wading flooding grassflats the best bet for reds.

Mangrove Shorelines

When there's enough water under the prop roots, reds like to creep through the tangle of mangrove legs. Weedless jerkbaits, weedless flies and floater/diver plugs work well in this situation. When the water is too low for reds to swim through the prop roots, they usually patrol the first slight dropoff, affording anglers great sight-fishing opportunities.

Low Country and North Florida Marshes

The biggest tides in redfish land occur from Northeast Florida, through South Carolina's Low Country to southern North Carolina. Six, even 8-foot tides push deep into the marshes, sometimes all the way to the oak hammocks that inhabit what little "high ground" there is. Fiddler crab colonies that are usually out of reach get flooded, and reds pile onto those flats and mop up the crustaceans. A handful of guides specialize in fishing these phenomenal events, and they pole up the small channels that flood and drain the flats as the fish move higher and higher onto the flat. Sometimes, they're rooting in water so shallow their backs are exposed. The editor of this book, Terry Gibson, will tell you about a fat Georgia red he'd stalked for half an hour, all the way to the edge of an oak hammock on Sapelo Island, only to watch the fish flee because of falling acorns.

"It's why I live here," says Savannah, Georgia guide and Shallow Water Angler regional editor Capt. Scott Wagner. "When a school gets up in the grass and starts feeding, it sounds like the public pool the day after school lets out. You usually get lots of shots, but the grass makes casting accurately such a challenge."

The trick is to use a weedless fly or lure just heavy enough to penetrate the jungle, but not too heavy or the splash will spook fish.

As these huge Low Country tides fall off a flat, anglers often find themselves beating a hasty retreat for deep

Top, during an incoming tide, expect reds to push back into creeks and onto flats. Below, the same creek at low tide. Expect fish to wait in ambush at the mouth.

water. If you're not careful, the water will disappear from under your boat.

As the water leaves the marsh, reds that still have an appetite take up ambush spots first in the shallow creeks that drain the marsh and then where they pour out into open water. Working the marsh drains with weedless flies or jerkbaits is usually quite rewarding.

Oyster Bars

Northeast Florida and the Low Country marshes also sport massive fields of oyster bars. At high tide, many areas look tranquil and interrupted as mill ponds. But as the tide falls out, massive oyster reefs seem to rise from the earth. In places, these mounds create small creek canyons.

Redfish take advantage of the incoming tide as it re-inundates the muddy shallows. They leave deeper flats near channels and forage often to the maximum distance into the labyrinth that the tide allows. You'll find them tailing, rooting out crabs and worms from the oysters, or laid up next to a reef.

As the tide falls, the fish move out of the shallows, often feeding lazily as the current takes them back toward deep water. Sometimes they huddle in deeper basins and you can catch them five at a time. Or, you can ambush them at the marsh drains on the edge of deep water.

Seagrass Flats

Depending on how shallow a flat gets at low tide, reds may stay on the same flat all day. Generally, reds will push ever shallower onto a flat as the tide allows, if there is sufficient forage in the extreme shallows. As the tide drops, they generally feed off the flat, gravitating toward the shallow channels that drain it. The fish will generally creep on and off a flat from the same places, generally where there's a drain. At dead low tide, work the edges of channels along productive flats. At high tide, the fish may sit in sandy holes in the grass. SB

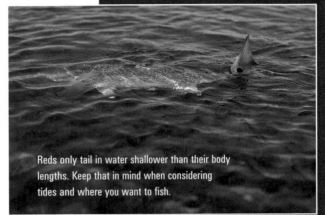

Reds only tail in water shallower than their body lengths. Keep that in mind when considering tides and where you want to fish.

CHAPTER 8

Structure

Habitat of some variety, usually a mix of different structures, is essential for any fishery. In some areas, a sustainable mix of natural habitat and manmade structure work together to enhance the productivity of an estuary or lagoon. Often, the best fishing occurs where two or more kinds of habitat occur in or close proximity, such as an oyster bar and mangrove stand, or under a dock surrounded by seagrasses.

During early life stages, newly settled and juvenile reds depend on seagrass, marsh meadows and shallow creeks. Their survival is obligated to these habitats. As older juveniles and adults, red drum have a "facultative" association with a wide variety of habitats. They aren't picky, and their wants are the same as most living things: safety, food, comfort and company.

Redfish are often found where two or more kinds of habitat create an edge or margin, one where food, safety, warmth or shade are close at hand, or fin.

See DVD for more on fishing structure.

Work areas carefully where natural and man-made structures coexist. Here reds pile up between the oyster bar and dock.

Hard Structure

Favorite rigid structures include jetty rocks, oyster reefs, worm and limestone reefs, and mangroves.

Redfish are predominately active foragers, but at times will wait in ambush just as snook and trout will. Reds often orient to hard structure, including oyster reefs, docks, jetties and bridges; as well as "soft" structure or contours including sand bars, marsh points and sod banks. Something as subtle as a lone oyster bar sticking up on a flat might harbor a fish or three. If there's an edge, or "margin" in scientific parlance, look closely and make a few casts.

Oyster Reefs

Oysters offer three vital ecosystem services to estuaries: filtration, habitat and protein. A single adult *Crassostrea virginica*, the Eastern oyster that occurs up and down the Eastern Seaboard, removes nutrients by filtering 60 gallons of water a day. Without these faithful bivalves, harmful algae blooms proliferate, among other consequences.

Except in hypersaline environments such as Texas' Lower Laguna Madre, oysters occur throughout the redfish's range. Where conditions are suitable, oysters create unique habitats as they build a type of biogenic reef. On biogenic reefs, structure is created by the animals themselves, versus reefs where animal and plant communities grow on raised or protruding rock. Typically, oyster spat (juvenile oysters) settle on rubble from old oyster beds or some other structure, then start to develop shells of their own or modify old shells to fit. Complex proteins called conchiolin are secreted from an

Nooks and crannies in oyster reefs hold a wide variety of prey that can be imitated with a number of flies. Conventional tackle is also appropriate.

oyster's outer epithelium or "mantle." Conchiolin holds and binds to crystals of aragonite, a type of calcium carbonate that precipitates or "falls" through the water column and is gathered by organisms such as oysters and corals.

When oysters grow in a colony, structure with incredible complexity or "rugosity" (literally, "wrinkled") is formed. Think of all the surface area that the sum of those shells creates in a very small total area, and think of all the interstitial nooks and crannies that provide habitat for almost everything that redfish like to eat. Worms, crabs, shrimp and blennies settle within or on the shells, while mullet graze on algae from the reefs.

In winter, focus on the sunlit side of mangrove shorelines with mud bottom, as they warm more quickly and heat triggers the appetites of cold, sluggish fish.

You might say that redfish love oysters because their beds are right next to the kitchen, as redfish relate to oyster reefs for both food and cover. Oyster bars located strategically at creek mouths, at the edge of a large flat or close to a mangrove edge often hold redfish.

The best time to map out a strategy for fishing oyster bars is during low tide, when most of the reefs are exposed and slight depressions in adjacent bottoms are revealed. Often a small mound of oysters that sticks out from the rest is a magnet. Bring a camera and GPS and take pictures of the flat at low tide. By studying the photos later, you will have a much better idea how redfish will relate to the oyster bars. You will also have a better idea of where to navigate without damaging the hull.

Depending on depth, clarity of water and available sunlight, you may or may not be able to sight fish. If you can't, a gold spoon or a small walking plug are great search lures. The spoon is relatively weedless, but make sure you don't let it fall into the oysters. Close your bail or stop your spool as soon as the spoon hits the water. Topwaters sure aren't weedless, but they do float over the snags. Work them a bit more slowly than you would for other predators.

Again, close the bail or stop the spool as the lure hits the water or the wind may blow the line onto exposed shells. Nicks and tangles are inevitable.

Mangroves

In tropical and subtropical climes, principally along the southern half of Florida and the southernmost shores of Texas, mangroves are keystone species. Three mangroves species occur in Florida, the red mangrove (*Rhizophora mangle*), black mangrove (*Avicennia germinans*) and white mangrove (*Laguncularia racemosa*). Black and white mangroves secure sediments that would otherwise cause turbidity on nearby grassbeds. They also serve as important rookeries for gorgeous birds such as roseate spoonbills and pelicans. By far the most important to estuarine life is the red mangrove, which typically grows along the water's edge. The red mangrove is identified by its tangled, reddish roots called "prop" roots. This network is deluxe fish habitat.

Mangroves are ecosystems unto themselves.

The importance of mangroves to a wide variety of marine life cannot be overemphasized. Mangroves provide protective nursery areas for fishes, crustaceans and shellfish. They provide habitat for the older juveniles of many species of snappers, grunts and groupers. They also provide food for a multitude of marine species such as snook, snapper, tarpon, jacks, sheepshead, oysters and shrimps, and of course red drum. Florida's important recreational fisheries would drastically decline if substantial losses of mangrove habitats continue.

Prop roots of red mangroves offer cover and hold favorite forage including pinfish and mojarra.

They trap and recycle various organic materials, chemical elements and important nutrients. The roots act as physical traps of mud and provide attachment surfaces for many marine organisms. Most of these attached organisms filter water through their bodies and, in turn, trap and cycle nutrients.

Redfish often cruise right through the prop roots along a mangrove shoreline. You can soak live bait under a popping cork just off a point, and wait for a fish to show up. Or, you can toss topwater plugs, flies, jigs and spoons up against the roots.

Rock Jetties

From Texas to North Carolina, rock jetties that protect deep passes offer redfish excellent structure and habitat. Big redfish (usually called "bulls") school at the very ends of rock jetties, or where scattered jetty rocks run out into the open ocean or Gulf waters. Holes or depressions indicate where passing storms have destroyed sections of the jetty rocks and relocated them nearby on the bottom. Slack tides aren't much good for jetty fishing, but it's hard to make a good presentation with a rampaging tide. The start of the flood or ebb is often the best time to fish these manmade structures. Look for bait. If you don't see birds diving on bait or birds sitting over bait, the fish likely aren't there. Next step is to consult your fish finder.

A wide variety of baits and lures work well around jetties.

During the mullet run, stick a ⅛- or ¼-ounce jighead through a finger mullet's lips. A knocker rig with a circle hook is also a great way to fish a live finfish or large crab. Circle hooks increase hookups and reduce mortality among released fish as they almost always stick in the corner of a fish's mouth. Large swimbaits work well in deeper waters and in current. Big lipped plugs do the dirty work below, but keep in mind that during shrimp and baitfish runs reds will merrily emerge from deep water to bash a surface lure.

Calm days make jetty fishing easy. Wear spikes when rocks are slippery.

Bridges

Bridges near inlet mouths, such as Florida's famous A1A bridge over Sebastian Inlet, and bridges over tidal creeks, offer shade and excellent ambush points. At the convergence of water bodies, changing water temperatures attract a variety of baitfish. Bridge supports also cause a "washtub" effect, which confuses baitfish schools, making them an easy target for redfish.

Some experts like to run the entire side of a bridge first with the fishfinder on to look for concentrations of baitfish and deep channels that move both baitfish and redfish through the manmade structure. During a falling tide, fish often lurk below the edge where the current is pushing from the deep channel over the shallow ledge. During an incoming tide, fish often hang above the dropoff where the current is pushing from the shallow ledge into the deep channel.

A bridge may offer excellent fishing during a particular tide on one day, and then the next day you might strike out. Keep in mind that bridges are often transitional structures where redfish pause when migrating between shallows and deeper open waters.

Boat Docks

Docks are great structures for redfish, particularly during low-tide phases. The very end of a boat dock is normally located where nearby shallow water drops off into a deep channel. At low tide, redfish will often hold under the end of a boat dock. At high tide, especially during the summer, reds will hold in the shade closer to shore, at whatever depth offers comfortable water temperature.

Boat docks with a nearby oyster bar, creek mouth, marsh point or perhaps simply a neigh-

Bridges confuse bait and create eddies. Reds stack up in the tide-worn sloughs between pilings.

Dock structure punctuates natural marsh. Combined manmade and natural habitats create extremely cozy margins for red fish. Work the docks thoroughly.

boring dock that extends further out into the channel seem to attract more redfish. In many areas, there may only be one out of several docks that consistently attracts redfish.

Dock fishing is a great venue for fly anglers, as a good caster can sling a fly sidearm way up under the dock. The long fly rod also helps leverage the fish out from the pilings. When working plugs around docks, baitcasting or plug tackle is preferable, since you can stop the lure on a dime simply by pressing down on the spinning spool. But arguably the best way to work a dock is by skip-casting a soft-plastic bait into the shade. Skip-casting is best accomplished with spinning tackle, as plug reels tend to overrun when the bait strikes the surface the first time. You have to cast sidearm, so that the lure strikes the water flat on its side about two rod lengths away from the boat, depending on the distance to the target. It takes a little practice, but works wonders in any kind of overhanging structure.

Soft Structure

Submerged or emergent fish habitats aren't necessarily hard structures. Seagrasses create a soft but complex web of cover that also holds abundant forage. Emergent marsh grasses create edges and harbor fiddler crabs. Reds also like to hunker down in soft mud, such as the alluvial sediments in Louisiana marshes. Finally, reds often herd baitfish onto shoals and sandbars, especially ebb and flood shoals inside or outside inlets and passes. The bronze fish are readily visible over white bottom.

Mud Flats

During winter and early spring, mud flats are a magnet for redfish. The winter sun can warm a dark, shallow flat much more quickly than a white sand flat. And the mud in turn warms the water, especially toward the bottom. Redfish typically enjoy their winter mud baths in very large groups, presumably as a safety in numbers strategy, as they are vulnerable to

Roseate spoonbill forages on a mud flat at low tide.

attack from above. So many sentinels, so many eyes make it hard to approach a school without spooking it. If you can't make out the edge of the school, you run the risk of beaning a fish with what seemed to be a bull's-eye cast to another fish in the school. And at times, especially when it's freezing cold, redfish will stick

their heads into the mud and steadfastly ignore lures or even bait.

Those stubborn fish may develop an appetite at the start of the incoming tide. Fly anglers who take care not to line the school while fixated on a single fish, catch the most fish. A small fly delicately presented is the best way to go. Small skimmer jigs, and small scented soft-plastics work best for spinning tackle.

Grassflats

Seagrasses are an essential component of a healthy estuary. Grassflats filter and purify saltwater, and shrimp, crabs, mullet and a variety of finfish make their homes on grassflats throughout the red drum's range. Because of the wide abundance and distribution of forage across a grassflat, redfish do more roaming and foraging here than ambushing.

Reds typically orient to holes in the seagrass, to shallow depressions, and to channels running through or along a flat. The conditions are so varied on open grassflats your tactics must be adapted to the situation at hand. If you can't sight fish, prospect with plugs and spoons. If the fish are shallow and the bottom firm, get out and wade, or pole stealthily.

meadows. When scared, a fish bolts or simply hunkers down and disappears.

Marsh Points

Never overlook a marsh point. As the tides rise and fall, redfish use marsh points as landmarks. Points extending out into a deep depression, sand hole, grassflat or river channel are especially attractive. The most effective way to fish a point is to stick a live finfish or shrimp under a cork right at the end of it. Or, systematically work plugs, jigs and flies.

Sand Bars

Sand bars or shoals, especially near inlet mouths, are always worth a look. Redfish may set up on the deep side of the bar waiting for some of their favorite forage to wash over. Sandbars also create a washtub effect, where swirling, sudsy currents confuse baitfish and make them an easy prey. In some regions, sand isn't part of the equation. In the Mississippi River Delta, reds orient to mud humps instead of sand shoals. Remember, big fish like big meals. Large swimming plugs and swimbaits work well on shoals.

Work shoreline leading up to marsh points and the points themselves. Below, sandbars near inlets offer light-bottomed venues.

CHAPTER 9

Artificial Lures

A huge variety of lures and flies, many adapted from bass fishing, allows you to work the entire water column for redfish in dozens of creative ways. Some lures, especially walking plugs (a.k.a. stickbaits) and spoons, have undergone more than 100 years of evolution.

For decades, bucktail jigs, especially the skimmer variety, were the go-to subsurface lure. Nylon was introduced but bucktail and chicken hackles remained the favorites. But in the last 15 years, innovations in soft-plastic baits have eclipsed hair jigs. Soft-plastic tails in many sizes, colors and shapes can be used on variously shaped and weighted jigheads, or rigged weedless on worm hooks, allowing an angler to work a lure at any reasonable depth, in strong or slack current, or in "tough neighborhoods."

Flies also have undergone tremendous refinements. The stalwart impressionist patterns, the Deceivers and Clousers, still catch 'em, and always will. But there are superbly accurate life-like imitations of crabs and shrimps that work best for smart fish.

The majority of lures, and to a lesser degree flies, were adapted from bass fishing.

REDFISH

See DVD for more on artificial lures.

Redfish are opportunistic feeders.
A variety of jigs, plugs, spoons
and flies work at different levels
in the water column.

The Artificial Advantage

A greater sense of accomplishment comes from catching redfish on flies or artificial lures.

These days, most places anyway, artificial lures and flies take more redfish than bait. Because of tremendous refinements in artificials—especially in lifelike scented soft-plastic baits, artificial lures and flies—in the right hands, can outperform natural offerings. While you may be able to procure one or two kinds of natural bait, you can load your

spoons and spinnerbaits, are great "search" lures. You can cast them a long way, and swim the lure across a lot of real estate until you find the fish.

With lures you can pick up after a bad cast much more quickly and with greater stealth than with live bait. Plus, lures rarely fall off the hook. Fly fishing, you can pick up the line immediately and cast again.

Finally, a greater sense of accomplishment goes along with tricking a redfish into eating something counterfeit. Catching a fish on bait is only a matter of getting dinner in a red's field of view or scent. Catching one on a fly or lure requires a good presentation, the skills to work the fly or lure in a convincing way and the experience to know when to set the hook.

tackle box with an assortment of artificials and flies that closely imitate wounded mullet, whitebait, shrimp, crabs—virtually anything a redfish eats. And lures don't die in the well. Sometimes, reds are keyed in a particular type of forage; maybe not what's in your baitwell. But the right lure can match the hatch perfectly.

Artificial lures and flies also allow an angler to cover more water than he might while soaking bait. Many lures, especially walking and swimming plugs,

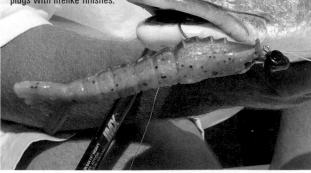

Scented soft baits, such as the Gulp! shrimp, provide the durability of plastic with the allure of real bait. At top are hard-body plugs with lifelike finishes.

With their underslung jaws, redfish almost look silly chasing down a topwater plug. They have a hard time grabbing the thing. Keep the plug moving until the fish succeeds.

Artificial Plugs

Topwater walking plugs and swimming plugs make great "search" lures. They cover a lot of water. Diving plugs, as well as suspending plugs, also allow an angler to work a finite area very thoroughly, since you can just about work these lures in place. Crankbaits send out all kinds of good vibrations and reds will come charging across a flat to attack one. A good redfisherman keeps a few of each type of plug in the box, and has a number of tricks up the sleeve for working each lure optimally.

Surface Plugs

Plugs with a cup-shaped face to make a popping sound have landed plenty of reds over the years. Some examples include Storm Chug Bug, Rebel Chug-R and Pop-R, Mirrolure 44MR and Trader Bay Trout Slayer. Propbaits, plugs equipped with one or two metal propellers that turn on the surface for a similar effect, also have fooled a red or two. Examples include the Smithwick Devil's Horse, Heddon Torpedo, and the MirrOlure 5M-28. But for reds, most experts favor "walking" plugs over all others. These plugs slash from side to side with rhythmic twitches of the rodtip, alternating slack and tight line during the retrieve. They bring to mind the movement

Big, noisy walking plugs work well in rough water; small baits work on glass. Below, loop knots accentuate action.

fast and with so little warning the strike jars the wrist. Hang on tight.

of a hyper dog on the end of a leash, hence the term for action, "walking the dog."

Smaller walking plugs are generally favored because redfish have a very hard time feeding on top due to their small mouths and underslung jaws. Smaller plugs fit in their jaws bet-ter and are less likely to spook a fish in shallow water. Examples include the Rapala Skitterwalk, Heddon Zara Spook, MirrOlure Top Dog, She Dog and She Pup, Rebel Jumpin' Minnow and Lucky Craft Saltwater Sammy.

Diving Plugs

Slim, lipped minnow-shaped diving plugs that wiggle on the retrieve are more popular for trout than reds, but redfish nail 'em. The floating versions work well around oyster bars and over pocked grassflats.

One deadly tactic is to make the plug dive and resurface repeatedly over a sandy hole on a grassflat. Many varieties are on the market, including the Rebel Minnow, MirrOlure L52MR, Cotton Cordell Red Fish, Bomber Long 'A', and several incarnations of the venerable Rapala. This category also covers jointed surface plugs such as the Rebel Jointed Minnow, which work well for bull reds in the surf, in and around passes and on shoals.

Top, crankbaits send vibrations through water as they cover real estate. Bottom, an assortment of favorite diving plugs and crankbaits.

Suspending Plugs and Crankbaits

Many of these lures resemble floater/diver slim minnows in shape and action, but are instead designed to sink slowly. A tight swimming action with a steady retrieve can be used (hence, "crank"), or a darting twitch. They're good in water from 3 to 6 feet, and deadly for working a piece of structure slowly and methodically. The Yo-Zuri Crystal Minnow, a number of Rapala plugs, the Rat-L-Trap series, the Bagley crankbait series and Sebile Stick Shad are typical of this class.

Sinking Plugs

Sinking plugs, sometimes called "twitch-baits," are much like suspending plugs except they have better depth capabilities, but lack the lip and built-in swimming motion. They can be made to twitch or dart attractively, cast or trolled. They're also very good for working structure slowly and methodically. Varieties include the soft Corky series, MirrOlure MirrOdine, the venerable 52M MirrOlure and the MirrOlure Catch 2000.

Sinking plugs work great along shorelines when the sun is high.

Suspending plugs shine around finite areas of structure. They stay in the strike zone longer.

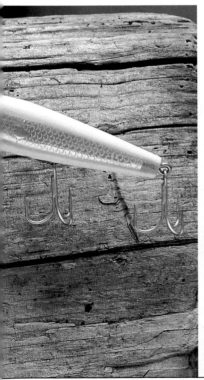

Rattles Attract

Rattles can either attract fish or scare the heck out of them. One of the best ways to find redfish that are hunkered down on a flat is to work the flat with an obnoxiously loud topwater. The fish will either attack it or flare off it. Either way, you know where they are.

Rattling plugs really produce in noisy conditions, such as a heavy chop. The rattles also add weight which translates to more casting distance. In swimming plugs, they sound a constant signal. In suspending plugs, they only "call" fish when the plug is twitched.

It's important to keep a variety of rattling plugs in the box, some subtle, some shrill, for a variety of water and "hatch" conditions. SB

Heavy Metal

Spoons are classic redfish lures adapted from bass fishing. The most popular spoon is the venerable Johnson Silver Minnow and modern variations. These spoons cast easily and are weedless, thus they work well for covering large, grassy areas. Because they skip well, some anglers like to use them under overhanging structure, such as mangrove limbs. Bright spoons stand out on bright days and dark spoons, even black spoons, are the call on dull days. Adding a plastic curly tail to a spoon is so productive it should almost be illegal.

Spoons

Probably more redfish have been caught on spoons than any other lure. Most commonly used for flats fishing are the single-hook spoons equipped with a weedguard. A moderately fast straight retrieve imparts a flashy wobble, but sometimes the fish will prefer a jigging action or a slower retrieve to crawl it through the grass. They're very popular lures on shallow grassflats and around oyster bars. They also are great search lures because you can cast them a mile. Gold and silver are popular colors, and some anglers like red. Attach the spoon to a snap swivel, which enhances action and reduces line twist. Examples include the classic Johnson Silver Minnow, the Bagley Rattl'n Minnow spoon, Red Ripper and Capt. Mike's Weedless Willow.

Spinner Baits

Many redfish lures and tactics were adopted from bass fishing. The spinnerbait is a shining example. A favorite in Gulf marshes, spinnerbaits are great search lures. Species such as snook and trout tend to shy away from them, so they're great if you're specifically targeting reds. A favorite is the safety-pin style. Safety-pin spinners employ a bent arm that suspends one or more blades over a skirt-tipped jighead. An in-line spinnerbait has a straight wire extending from the head with a spinner rotating around the wire. A beetle spinner, also known as a "harness" spinner, resembles a safety-pin spinnerbait, but it usually consists of a wire harness temporarily

Redfish number 1,000,001 caught on a wobbling spoon.

attached to a standard lead jighead. Many anglers attach scented soft plastics for added appeal. Nearly round "Colorado" blades and light jigheads work best in shallow water. In deeper water, opt for willow-shaped blades with heavier jigheads. Popular spinnerbaits include the Bagley series, Bayou Buck series and the Beetlespin series.

Spoons and spinnerbaits are great blind-casting lures. They're tough to beat for fan casting an open flat or working a shoreline.

Nature Fakers

Whether fishing in 6 inches of water or 60 feet, jigs are primarily used for bottom work. Most shallow-water applications involve bouncing a jig along the bottom, generally at a slower pace when the water is exceptionally warm or cold. Skimmer-type jigs ride upside down and are virtually weedless. Tipping one with shrimp makes it even more weedless, and sweeter. Soft-plastic jig tails allow an angler to change presentations quickly, to match the dominate forage. Plus, they feel real and a fish will hang on to a soft-plastic bait longer than a bucktail. There's a jig for every occasion.

Bucktail Jigs

This category also includes jigs tied with nylon, feathers, Mylar and other fibrous materials. White, yellow, brown and char-

Hair jigs of various weights are ideal from flats to deep channels.

treuse are popular colors. Flattened skimmer-type jigs are the most popular for shallow reds, as the hookpoint rides up, snagging less grass. Other head shapes such as the pom-pano, ball, bullethead and lima bean, are designed to hop or dart through the water column. Quarter- to 3/8-ounce models are typically used. Heavier bucktails from 1/2- to 3/4-ounce can be used for probing channels, inlets and offshore livebottom. Add a bit of shrimp or cutbait if you like.

Soft-Plastic Jerkbaits

Descendents of freshwater bass worms, soft-plastic jerkbaits can be rigged completely weedless, which is especially helpful on shallow grassflats and around mangroves or oyster shells. They're also great in super-skinny water, as the lures hit the water softly by virtue of their light weight and trim profile. Heavier bodies feature a hook pocket.

Customization options include bullet weights, plastic rattles, and paint-on or insert eyes. Makers include those mentioned under Plastic-Tail Jigs, as well as Bass Assassin, Cotee, Culprit and Lunker City. **SB**

"Worm" hooks for different size jerkbaits range from No. 3/0 to No. 7/0.

Plastic-Tail Jigs

Plastic-tail jigs are suitable for the same applications as bucktail jigs. Several styles of soft-plastic tails can be added to naked jigheads, opening up a world of customization options. Choices include curly tails, shad tails and flap tails. Pradco offers a tail that can be customized for depth and flutter by tearing out a piece of the tail along a perforated edge. Some plastics offer built-in scent. Jigheads are most commonly sold in 1/8- to 3/8-ounce weights. Popular soft-plastics or products made of other soft materials are made by D.O.A., Berkley Gulp!, Pradco, Floriday's Fishing, Hogy, Hookup Lures, Bagley, Riptide, Old Bayside and Cotee.

Lifelike Soft Plastics

This category includes soft-plastic lures designed to precisely imitate natural prey. Popular designs mimic shrimp, myriad crabs and a variety of baitfish. They are excellent for sight casting in very clear water, and in nearly all cases, a slow retrieve works best. They can also be effective fished under a popping cork. Examples include the Sea Bay Shrimp and Crab, D.O.A. Shrimp, Crab, Baitbuster and TerrorEyz, Gulp!, Pradco Houdini Crab, Carolina Lures Sandflea and Cotee.

Soft-plastic bodies imitate shrimp, marine worms, crabs—you name it. They can be fished Texas-style, or on jigheads.

Soft-plastic crabs work well for shallow, stealthy applications.

Weights can be attached to the hook for more casting distance, better grass penatration and more jig-like action.

Redfish Flies

Stalking big, smart fish in the shallows, fly anglers enjoy the best stealth advantage.

Fly fishing may be the most difficult form of fishing to master, but it's also the most versatile tackle. A range of lines, from heavy-sink to floating, allow you to cover the entire water column. Rods with slower and faster actions facilitate casting sinking or floating lines. But the flies themselves provide an angler with the most versatility. From "mortar Clousers" that plumb the depths of inlets and passes, to suspending crab patters that hover tantalizingly in inches of water, flies can do it all.

The subject of redfish fly patterns could easily fill a book of its own. In general, surface baitfish imitators include deerhair sliders, Muddler Minnows, Dahlberg Divers and foam-

Hair bugs, poppers, Diver, Crease Fly and Gurgler.

or cork-bodied poppers. A favorite is the soft foam popper called the Gartside Gurgler. Mid-water streamers include Lefty's Deceivers, Bendbacks, Norm's Crystal Schminnow, Glass Minnows, the Eat Me and many others.

Dupree spoon flies are an essential in any redfish fly box. Crustacean imitations designed to be fished on or very near the bottom run the gamut from attractors such as the black Clouser Minnow to lifelike Merkin crabs. It should be noted that fly anglers enjoy a special advantage when reds are targeting very small prey such as tiny anchovies or shrimp. Fly fishing is also a stealthier approach when sight-fishing calm, shallow water. SB

Top, Lefty's Deceivers and PolarFibre Minnows flies are two of the most successful baitfish patterns. Bottom, Bendbacks are weedless and work well in grass. Merkin and other precise crab patterns fool smart fish.

CHAPTER 10

Natural Baits

Anglers sight casting to spooky reds on clear, shallow flats use tail-hooked or Texas-rigged live shrimp because the splash is minimal and scent dispersal immediate. Live or cracked crab also works in that situation. When drifting flats or working marsh points, a popping cork attracts reds, keeps bait at a specific level in the water column and serves as a strike indicator.

Live chumming is controversial because in places overuse of the practice has created "Pavlov's reds." But when the fishing is tough it's a great way to attract reds. Typically, "whitebait" of some variety is used. Live finger mullet are a favorite bait in inlets and passes. Fish them on jigheads or under fishfinder rigs. Freelining a live finger mullet around jetty rocks and oyster rakes can also be deadly.

Dead bait shines in places where you know that reds will show up eventually—a channel draining a flat, an outer bar or a deep hole outside the inlet. The downside to dead bait is that pests such as sharks, skates and catfish may beat reds to the offering.

Strong high-pressure systems tend to make redfish really skitzy and give them a bad case of lockjaw. Switch to cut bait given such conditions.

See DVD for more on natural baits.

The sign says it all. Reds
prefer shrimp and crabs,
but will eat croakers,
typically used for trout.

LIVE BAIT SHRIMP
6 14. 00 qt   6 7. 00 pt
DEAD BAIT SHRIMP 9 2 00 ft
ICE   Bag
CROAKERS $3.50 Doz.

LIVECRABS $10 00 dozen

LIVE
CROAKER

Dirty "Stinking" Tactics

Mojarra, pinfish, pigfish and mullet are important parts of a red's diet. But red drum feed primarily on crustaceans, worms and bivalves.

The democratic diets and feeding habits of red drum allow for just about any style of light-tackle fishing. Live and dead baits, as well as a wide variety of artificial flies and lures all have their application or applications. A good angler picks the right horse for the course.

Blue crabs live in seagrass and in sandy edges and potholes near seagrass meadows. They keep flats clean and provide predators with protein.

several smaller baits, and a hunk of blue crab may be the best of all baits for giant bull reds in Florida's northern Banana River and Mosquito Lagoon. There, the strategy is to throw half a crab ahead of the school and let those big, lazy fish wander over and scarf it up. Remove the top shell and claws. Cut the crab into four baits. Take a 4/0 red circle hook and barb the crab right through the shell and fish the bait dead on the bottom. In shallow sloughs, chunks of blue crab are effective when fished without any weight. In deep water or deeper sloughs, fish chunks of blue crab on a sliding sinker fishfinder rig. Here's one way to do it:

First slide an appropriately sized egg sinker onto your line, followed by a small plastic bead. Next, tie on a

Crabs

Stick your finger down a redfish's throat, into the crushers, and you'll get a good idea of what they eat—crabs. (We don't recommend trying on a live specimen—ouch!) Crabs are a principle component of a redfish's diet, and they feed on all sorts of crabs including blue crabs, fiddler crabs and mole crabs (sandfleas). Most anglers prefer blue crabs for bait, since fiddler and other species are much smaller. Clip the pinchers off a smaller blue crab before putting a 2/0 circle hook through the side of the shell, or the crab may exact a little revenge. Quarter-sized live blue crabs are great for sight casting to really spooky fish in skinny water. They also work well under popping corks.

A good-size blue crab can be broken into

Live crabs work well for spooky reds and under popping corks.

50-pound-test barrel swivel: the palomar knot is good for this, but a uni-knot works fine also. Finally, tie a 3-foot section of 50-pound fluorocarbon shock leader to the other end of the barrel swivel and to the eye of the circle hook, again using palomar knots. You can modify the components as you like, and of course use whatever knots you are comfortable tying.

Fish the chunk of blue crab dead on the

bottom. You can place the rod in a rod holder, but some prefer to hold it, making sure the crab bait stays on the bottom and also to detect a redfish strike.

When a redfish picks up the crab, it will first move the bait back into its mouth, then crush the crab with its huge molars. Wait patiently until the redfish tightens up your fishing line, and then apply steady pressure to the rod. The circle hook will move from the back of the mouth to the corner of the mouth, making for a perfect hookset. More importantly, this will avoid hooking the redfish in the throat, or worse yet, in the stomach.

There's no better way to introduce new anglers to redfishing than with a live shrimp dangling under a popping cork.

Shrimp

One of the more popular techniques is fishing live shrimp under a rattling float. Sometimes called a "Cajun float," this style of float has a large wire running through the float with beads attached to both ends of the wire. The bottom of the float also has a weight threaded on to the wire, which allows longer casts and makes the float stand straight up when fished.

Attach the non-weighted end of the float to your terminal fishing line, using a palomar knot. Next, attach a 2-foot section of 20-pound fluorocarbon shock leader to the weighted side of the float. Finally, add a No. 4 Kahle hook to the tag end of the shock leader.

First break the horn of the shrimp off; this allows for a better hookset. Next, barb the live shrimp right in front of the dark spot located on the top of the head. Cast the float and live shrimp combo toward a promising piece of water, and occasionally jerk the float. The popping noise it makes on the surface mimics the sound of redfish eating shrimp. It's a sure bet for attracting fish to your bait.

When a redfish takes the shrimp, first allow it to swim the slack out of the line, then—and only then—set the hook. If the float goes under and simply sits there, reel in the slack and set the hook.

Louisiana fishermen often use fresh dead shrimp when fishing with this same rattling float setup. In this case they barb the dead shrimp through the meat of the tail. When the float is jerked, the dead shrimp actually looks as if it is trying to escape the jaws of a hungry redfish.

One trick when using live shrimp is pinching, cutting or even biting off the tail of a live shrimp. For sight fishing, take a No. 1 Kahle hook, or a 3/0 red circle hook and barb the shrimp in the remaining tail section. Or, turn the hook over once you pierce the tail and

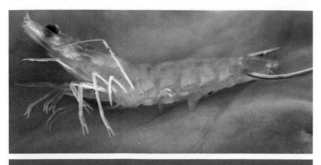

with a 7-foot, 6-inch spinning rod. Fill your reel with 10-pound braided line and attach a 3-foot section of 20-pound fluorocarbon shock leader. The shock leader may be attached to the braided line using a uni-knot. Tie the leader to the hook with a palomar knot. With this setup, you'll be able to cast the shrimp right in front of a school of redfish, even on a windy day.

Above, tail-hooked live shrimp appear to flee when popped by the angler. Below, bite the tail off to Texas-rig live shrimp.

This same setup can also be fished with a fishfinder setup, described in the section on fishing blue crabs. Use the appropriate size egg sinker in order to keep the live shrimp on the bottom.

One last live shrimp rig worth mention involves tying a ¼-ounce leadhead jig to the end the shock leader. Next, barb the live shrimp just in front of its tail,

Texas-rig the bait, if grass or weeds are an issue. Pinch a splitshot sinker onto the line just ahead of the hook for added casting distance.

This setup is especially deadly when fished

starting under the tail and right out through the top. Swim the live bait slowly along the bottom. This is often referred to as "slow jigging".

Other Finfish and Cutbait

Other popular live baits include menhaden, croaker, pinfish, whiting, "greenbacks" and cocahoe minnows, also called bullheads. You can rig up much as you would with a mullet; just change hook sizes to match the size of the bait.

Cocahoe minnows, left, are popular in the Low Country. White bait, above, is choice on the lower Gulf Coast.

Two final baits that are very effective for redfish, but sometimes difficult to secure, are fresh squid and shrimp mammies (mantis shrimp). Fresh local squid fished with a fishfinder setup right on the bottom is a deadly tactic. Shrimp mammies are like a crustaceous dinosaur with their spiny shell. Redfish simply love them. In some regions, both shrimp mammies and squid can be obtained from local shrimp boats and when freshly netted, these make perfect bottom bumping baits for redfish. SB

Mullet

Fishing with live mullet often entices the largest of redfish to eat. As a bait supply, mullet are usually easier to obtain than crabs and can be fished using a variety of techniques. During the fall mullet run, look for a shallow flat or bar where mullet are running and the reds will be near.

One good mullet technique is to use the same fishfinder setup mentioned earlier. Barb the baitfish through the bottom of the mouth and right out through the top of its head. Cast and wait for that solid strike that is certain to happen. Once a redfish has eaten the live finger mullet, wait for a slow count of five, tighten up the line and set the hook.

Live silver mullet, and finger mullet below are caught with castnets and fished under corks or freelined on circle hooks.

When fishing for redfish weighing to 10 pounds, the perfect bait is a 4- to 5-inch mullet. Larger reds will take larger live mullet, measuring from 6 to 10 inches. SB

Mullet Chunks

Cut chunks of mullet and strips of mullet also work well for redfish and are an excellent choice when the water is discolored. The smell of the cut mullet is very attractive to foraging redfish. Other cut baits that work well include croaker, whiting, bluefish, menhaden and ladyfish. Once again, fish cut baits with the same fishfinder setup described earlier.

Strips of mullet make the best surf-fishing baits and can also "stink" out elusive redfish from the flats and channels.

CHAPTER 11

Tactics

Redfish tactics are highly varied. Often a tactic is dictated by the circumstances. For example windy weather and open flats call for drift fishing. Glass calm days and skinny water call for stealthier approaches, usually poling or wading. The deep, swift waters of passes and inlets may call for anchoring. A depression or channel through a flat may call for staking out.

Different flies, lures and tackle lend themselves to each scenario. A baitcasting outfit and spinnerbait or spoon covers the most water while drifting. A light spinner and ¼-ounce skimmer jig may be the call in slick shallows. Staking out, you can put the boat well within fly-casting range of the anticipated targets. In the passes, stout spinners and conventional reels shoulder the burden of heavy lead. Each of these ways to fish is a challenge, and a blast.

Targeting redfish will take you through America's most complex, beautiful estuaries and nearshore waters.

See DVD for more on redfishing techniques.

White pelicans share forage preferences with red drum, such as shrimp, killifish and other small fish. Bird activity is always a good sign. In fact, foraging birds of many varieties make great "native guides."

Sight Fishing

Sight fishing for reds ranks highest on the list of most exciting and most technical of fishing strategies. Those blue-tinged rosy tails waving in early morning or late-afternoon light have caused divorces, fir-ings and career changes, as well as incited tournament mania. But whether sight fishing on foot or from a poling skiff, or blind casting while drifting or moving along via trolling motor, fishing for redfish requires a wide variety of technical skills.

Tailing Reds

Redfish "tail" when they tip down to root shrimp, crabs, worms and other forage from the

bottom in water shallower than the length of the body. Tailing occurs as redfish move further back onto the flooding marsh, mud flat, or sandbar where the water depth is super shallow. Redfish also tail as they follow the falling water off of a flat. In fact, redfish may tail at any time during the day, depending on water depth, forage source and water temperature. But the tails tend to wag more happily in low light, which obviously presents a problem for sight fishermen. You can only see the fish while the tail is exposed, and you can't easily tell if and where other fish are in relation to the one with its tail in the air. So, you run the risk of spooking the entire school with what you thought was a good presentation. It's all part of the game.

Getting a shot requires stealth; making the shot requires pinpoint casting accuracy. The best time to make your presentation is when the tail's up and the fish's head is down in the grass, sand or mud. Tailing reds can be downright

Kayaks are the ultimate stealth craft, and feet make great breaks. 'Yaks let you get really close to tailing fish. Just make sure not to throw a shadow over the fish with the rod or line.

oblivious, or at least far less likely to spook when your offering hits the water. Just make sure not to hit the fish with the lure or line.

You can tell which way the red is facing by the angle of the tail. Think of the tail as the quills of an arrow. The business end is facing in the opposite direction. Your presentation should generally land about a foot to 18 inches from the fish's nose. Often they'll grab the bait on

Both to protect your eyes and see fish, polarized sunglasses are the most important investment. They are windows into the soul of an estuary.

Reds often use creeks that connect bayous or bays as highways. Even subtle grass points make good ambush spots.

the fall. If not, give the lure, fly or bait the slightest motion. If fishing with spin or plug tackle, just turn the reel a half turn and the lure will create a small, attracting puff. If fly fishing, move the fly with a 1-inch strip. If that doesn't get the fish's attention, pop the lure or fly off the bottom. If these tactics fail to entice a strike, but the fish or school doesn't flare off either, wait very quietly for a few minutes and a single fish or the school may resume tailing.

High Sun

Sight fishing doesn't necessarily entail casting to tailing fish. In fact, fish are less likely to tail when the visibility is best, presumably because that's when they're most vulnerable to

aerial assaults from large birds. On sunny days, the best sight-fishing conditions occur between 10 a.m. until 2 p.m., when the sun is the highest and offers optimum visibility in the shallows. At this time of the day, fish are more likely to be lying in the mud or in grass than tailing, but you can see them.

Sight fishing with a high sun is a little more technical in that you must plan your approach to the flat to keep the sun at your back. It is difficult to sight fish for redfish while looking directly into the sun. Bright light demands intense concentration. Stalk with your pores open. Cast at anything that makes your senses suspect fish. Listen for splashes. Use your peripheral vision to detect movement, such as

Sunglasses for Sight Fishing

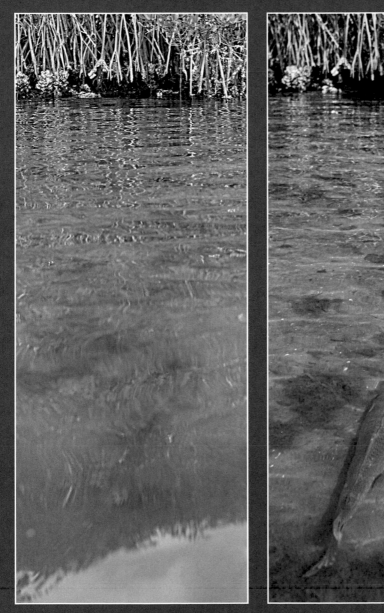

Premium polarized sunglasses are a must, and lenses with an amber or copper tint work best for flats fishing. Lightly tinted shades help pull out shapes from the water in low light. Side shields are helpful in terms of keeping the sun's rays from shining directly on the backside of your sunglasses, casting a reflection back into your eyes. Bring a good cleaning cloth or other non-abrasive material to keep your sunglasses clean and clear.

Overcast skies can be a blessing or

fleeing shrimp or baitfish. Keep your eyes moving and scan the shallow flats slowly—moving eyes will see a lot more than eyes that are standing still. Look for a redfish tail under water, as it sways back and forth. The blue-tinged tail, with a large dark spot or several spots, is easier to see than the body and head of the redfish. Use your active vision to discern fish shapes and determine the direction that the fish is facing; then cast appropriately. Make sure neither your shadow nor the shadow of the rod passes over the fish, or the fish will fly off that flat.

Inset, wading birds and tailing reds are often together. Work the discernible edges and potholes on overcast days.

Gray Light, Stained Water

It's a lot to ask for the right tide, feeding fish and good visibility. The right tide and to a lesser degree feeding fish can be predicted. Good viz is anything but predictable. Clouds, wind-churned water and tannin-stained runoff can individually or cooperatively make redfish very hard to see.

When the water is clear but the sun is behind clouds, a team of poling anglers has the best shot at success. The angler on the bow should look almost straight down, while the poling angler searches to the limit of the already limited field of view. If you're quiet, you can sneak right up on redfish.

When the water is stirred up, you must look for more subtle signs. The least subtle sign is when the surface simply erupts. A nervous shimmer may also indicate a large school. A fleeing shrimp or baitfish is a call for a cast to that area. Redfish may betray themselves by waking. These wakes are easy to identify—voluminous, consistent and move decidedly in one direction. Waking mullet are frequently mistaken for redfish, but nervous mullet swim erratically. Redfish wakes, sometimes referred to as "pushes," move at a steady pace and in the same direction.

urse. On summer days, fish will feed a little later and they're not as wary.

Poling

Poling skiffs give anglers a number of advantages. For one, the higher the platform, the better the view. These days, most poling takes place from a platform located above the outboard. Increasingly, anglers are installing casting platforms on the

Teamwork makes poling all the more rewarding. Both anglers deserve credit for the catch.

bow to help the caster better see fish. If you don't have a raised deck platform on the bow of your skiff, a sturdy cooler will give you a higher if tippy watchtower. Some nimble, thrifty anglers even carry along a 6-foot folding ladder.

In many cases, the angler on the poling platform will see the fish first and then attempt to point them out to the angler on the bow. The clock system is employed, with the center of the bow always represented as 12 o'clock. Distances are estimated, and a direction called out. If the bow angler still can't see the fish, the poler may point with the pushpole, if throwing a shadow can be avoided. Or, the poling angler takes the shot himself. Most poling platforms have rod holders mounted on one or both sides. Some anglers prefer to set the rod on the platform itself, between the legs, or just stick the rod butt in a pocket.

Staking out is another important poling skill. Drive the sharp end into the mud, but not at too high of an angle or you may shatter the pole. Loop a rope or bungee

The point of the bow is always 12 o'clock. Range is called out in feet

Poling is an incredibly exciting, even nerve-wracking way to fish. But the setting is almost always a picture of tranquility.

Steering Aid

When it comes to sneaking up on redfish in Florida's hard-fished Mosquito Lagoon, Mark Hatter is considered one of the best. Hatter keeps a small portion of the lower unit in the water so that his boat tracks better while poling.

It is important that his boat does not create a bow wave, or generate slapping noise. So, Hatter inches the boat forward. If the boat is poled too fast, even a hull designed to minimize disturbances will create noise.

In places where redfish are super spooky, such as the Mosquito Lagoon, fidgety redfish can sense the pressure of a boat moving through the water. That's also why Hatter inches his forward.

Finally, Hatter uses his hips as a fulcrum to help steer his boat while poling. If Hatter wishes to steer the bow to the starboard, he will push with his hips and pole to the left to steer to the right, and vice versa. SB

cord around the foot, and attach it to the poling platform. There are a variety of tools that help you secure the pole, including clips.

Stopping or slowing the boat is an impor-

Clips mounted along the side of a poling platform hold the pole firmly and quietly, in case the stern angler needs to take the shot.

Staking Out The Scene

Sometimes redfishing is like deer hunting: You motor up to a spot where your quarry is likely to cross, get up in your perch (in this case, the poling platform), wait for the sun (and tide) and watch for movement. Other times, you pole up stealthily into an area where you expect reds to show up and feed. Or you pole up on a school of reds and you want to stay put to let both anglers get a

tant skill when you're moving with wind or tide toward a body of fish. Especially when fly fishing, you want to turn the bow so that the angler is casting off the bow, and not over the boat. You can slow the boat by placing the pole amidships and pushing. How hard you push is a function of how quickly you want to slow the boat and turn the bow.

Learning to steer a skiff with a pushpole takes a bit of practice. In general, a push on the starboard side of the stern will push the bow in the same direction. Try not to switch sides often; rather push in the opposite direction with the pole behind your back. (You lose momentum when you switch sides too much.)

Reds are spotted, and the hydraulic pole is deployed while the trolling motor holds the bow against a grass edge.

shot. The pushpole can serve as an anchor. Set it in the bottom at a 20- to 45-degree angle to the water—just enough to grab and keep a bend under tension from tide or wind. Tie off at the bow or stern (usually stern) with a line or double bungee cord. Another option is a Power-Pole, a 22-pound hydraulic system mounted on the transom just above the waterline. It's operated by remote control. Press a button and an aluminum staff lowers quietly. You're staked out in about 8 sec-

onds. Power-Poles do a great job holding the boat in position, but occasionally, in a strong cross wind, the bow will swing. In such circumstances, pros deploy what's called a Cajun anchor from the bow. A Cajun anchor is a spear anchor. It slides vertically into the bottom and requires very little scope. Just make sure to deploy it on the upwind side of the bow. SB

In lieu of a hydraulic pole or pushpole, spear anchors hold the bow or stern in a fixed position.

Wade Fishing

Wade fishing fully immerses you in their world—makes you part of it.

Wade fishing is the stealthiest way to approach spooky reds, particularly when they are holding in shallow water and get a lot of pressure. You can wade in depths where the shallowest draft skiff is left high and dry. Or, when in Texas, you can wade in a line of anglers up to your neck.

Wading is arguably the best way to work a flat when fish aren't feeding aggressively

When sight fishing on foot, you may have more time to take the shot than from a boat. Don't over-think it.

and/or visible. A wading angler can take a few steps, fan cast 300 degrees, take a few more steps and do it again. Since you're fishing from a fixed platform—the bottom—wading also gives you the greatest control over the line and lure or fly. There's no boat to drift and drag the line, or creep up on it. You're also not depending on a partner or a buzzing electric motor to get you into position. You know how you cast best, from what angle you're most accurate. And you can wait as long as practical to take the shot. If you make a bad cast and the fish get wary, or whiff on the strike, you can simply let the fly or lure sit on the bottom until things settle down without worrying about drifting through the fish or off of them. Simply stand there until the fish resume feeding, or move on to a new pod.

Modern neoprene waders have given anglers a real advantage in cold weather. The warmth they provide has added fishable days to the calendar. Wintertime reds can be really sluggish, and it may be difficult to work a lure slowly enough unless you're wading. It's hard to fish patiently if you're uncomfortable.

Even in warm weather, waders can be a good idea, especially if you have cuts on your legs or feet. In rare cases anglers have succumbed to water-borne diseases, including staph infections and flesh-eating bacteria. If water quality is at all an issue where you live, or you're fishing Texas back bays that are notorious for such diseases, it's a good idea to wear waders.

The Essential and Optional Gear for Wading

A good pair of wading shoes with hard rubber soles is a must. Wading shoes that dry out fast are also a good option. The new rubber shoes with all of those big holes are perfect for wade fishing. The large holes allow the water and any sand to be flushed and dried in a hurry.

There are a couple of safety concerns associated with wading. One, make sure to test the bottom before you leave your fishing boat. Just because it looks solid doesn't mean that you won't sink to your neck. Second, look before you leap. Many a fishing trip has been ruined by jumping barefoot onto an unseen oyster shell, or worse, a stingray. On that subject, always shuffle your feet and try not to backtrack into your trail. Stingrays will follow you, feeding on the worms and crustaceans you dislodge as you walk.

Lightweight fishing pants offer some protection from jellyfish and other critters that can inflict pain to your exposed legs. A vest holds extra lures, pliers and other essentials while you are away from your boat or dry land. A bait bucket is a must for keeping baits lively and within easy reach. A small landing net tied to your belt will also aid in landing big redfish. SB

Wading belts hold tackle boxes, sport rod holders, and strap in water bottles. If you plan on keeping fish, use a rod holder to hold a net.

Floats prevent stringers of fish, pliers and other essential from being lost. If you're wading in a sharky area, keep your catch at a distance.

Top step, lightweight, breathable waders. Bottom step, wading shoes range from boots to wading shoes to booties to Kevlar "stickfish" boots.

Texas Waders

Wading is a great Texas tradition. Teams of anglers move in a line, often at different depths and fan cast an area. Often a float with drinks, creel, net and other gear drifts along with them. There's no better way to find fish.

Texans' love for wading produced a sub-genre of tackle designed to be efficient when you're up to the neck in water. Rods (generally baitcasters) for wading have short handles, so they're not sloshing in the water while you work the bait. They may also be a little longer than usual, to make up for the lack of elevation while casting and to add action to the lure.

Working a lure while wading, especially wading deep, takes some practice. On a boat, you can twitch a topwater, jerkbait or suspending plug moving the rodtip down and away. With the rodtip low, you're in a good position to set the hook. But if you're up to your chest, you have to keep the rodtip high. This angle exposes the line to drag from the wind, so you must anticipate the angle. Hooksetting is more difficult, and if you set the hook to hard with the tip straight up you may fall over backward. It takes a little getting used to, unless you grew up doing it.

Getting wet feels great on a hot summer day. Good thing that wading deep is one of the summer's most productive tactics.

Texas anglers search out fish working a series of subtle dropoffs at different depths. Right, this fish was about waist deep.

▶ Pro Tip Skinny Tipping

Chuck Howard of Bradenton, Florida, is a firm believer in wade fishing. His home waters are on Sarasota Bay.

"Sometimes we can't catch these 'city' reds from a boat, they are just too spooky," he says.

Chuck likes to work sand holes that finger

Stay in an athletic position and keep a low profile while stalking fish.

out into channels during the incoming tide, when the fish pour into the shallows. He likes ⅛-ounce lead jigheads, rigged White Exude Shad, or a ¼-ounce D.O.A. shrimp. He allows the bait to sit on the bottom for a few seconds before twitching it. Working the bait aggressively from the get-go is apparently a turnoff for spooky reds.

Drift Fishing

Drift fishing allows you to cover vast expanses of water. The trick is to drift at a speed and angle that allow for proper bait and lure presentations. You won't catch many fish racing your lure through the water column, nor with you drifting toward it so fast you can't keep out the slack.

Drift speed depends on current, wind and the boat's length, freeboard and windage, and draft. Near inlets, current will likely prevail.

Away from inlets, wind will usually be the prime mover. Remember that "wind blows from," and current "flows to." The forces work together, one prevails over the other or they can be moving at right angles. You need to anticipate the direction of the drift, although you don't need to be as accurate if you have a trolling motor.

When wind and tide oppose each other, you might not move much at all, which is perfect if you're in fish or working a specific feature. The challenge, when wind and tide work together, is drifting slowly enough. For inshore purposes, drift socks, or "drogues," range from 24 to 30 inches in diameter. (They range from $35 to $200 for the fully adjustable models.) Socks both slow the drift and take the bounce

Reading current and wind direction and factoring the relative influences of both aren't easy. "Getting the drift" has a learning curve.

Etiquette is important when there's "company." Move in quietly, without throwing a wake and mind the lines of others. Below, drift sock deployed from amidships.

out of a rocking boat. If it's really choppy and you're worried about hull slap spooking fish, deploy the sock from the bow. A bow-deployed sock really softens the bounce.

If you deploy a drift sock straight behind the boat, with the outboard straight, one or more anglers can fish from the bow. This deployment also allows you to use the trolling motor to maneuver left and right. Just be careful not to swamp the boat.

While bow-first is certainly the quietest drift, it's not the best use of the entire boat's fishing area. And, if you're dragging a bait behind the boat, you invite tangles with the drift-sock line. You can also deploy the sock from amidships, and turn the outboard hard in one direction or the other so that the boat "crabs" sideways. If the boat is long enough, three anglers can cast and a bait can be dragged from the bow or stern, far enough away from the sock to avoid tangling. Meanwhile, anglers cast ahead or at right angle of the drift direction.

One of the quietest ways to work a shoreline is to drift. Deploy the sock from the back corner of the windward side and use the trolling motor just enough to stay parallel to the shoreline.

Drift fishing is usually about covering water until you find fish. When you find fish, it's important to mark the bite. Anglers in smaller skiffs, kayaks and canoes can either stake out

Working a shoreline with the wind reduces hull slap. A drift sock helps control the drift.

WIND

DRIFT

The trolling motor maintains bow control and puts anglers in casting position.

with a pushpole or gently slip a bell anchor overboard and fish 'til the bite stops. Throw a big anchor over though, and the bite is bound to stop instantly. Another option is to hit the "man overboard" button on a GPS; drift through the fish, and then, making a wide swing, motor back updrift of the spot.

Kayaks will sail on you if there's a breeze. A sock and an understanding of the tide strength are important.

Electric Motors

Electric motors have become much quieter and fishermen have learned how to use them on super-low speeds without spooking redfish. They are essential for anglers who work long stretches of shorelines or blind-cast large flats.

The first and foremost requirement for using an electric motor is to adjust the height so that the blades do not hit the bottom. This not only destroys grasses but also spooks fish. At the same time, don't raise the motor so high that the propeller cavitates, which will

Elevation is useful when electric motoring down a shoreline. Left, a strap reduces pounding and the need for repairs.

also spook nearby fish. Finally, operate the motor on a steady, slow speed. Changing the speed from low to high also alerts fish to your presence.

When fan casting or working a bank while under electric motor, it's important to control the speed so you don't overtake the line or interfere with the angle or action of the lure. Reverse is one of a trolling motor's finest features, if it's employed gently. Slam on the breaks, so to speak, and you'll spook every red within a mile.

Every angler has reached for the trolling motor just as a fish strikes, and missed. Fly anglers have more of these stories than conventional anglers. Remote controls have reduced such incidents, but you still need to get the boat situated so that ideally you don't have to fiddle with the motor again until the fly or lure is retrieved.

Trolling motors seem like flyline magnets. There's not much you can do about line catching on the handle, except use a stripping basket or Line Tamer. But if the wind's light, you can throw a wet towel down on the deck and over the bracket.

Electric motors can also be used as "trolling" motors, as they are often called. With the electric deployed, you call troll live baits, plugs, spoons or jigs along promising shorelines or structure. SB

Cut 'Em Off at the Pass

You can use the electric motor to chase big fish. It's unlikely that a red drum would ever spool you. But when they break for structure, the electric allows you to cut the fish off at the pass. In deep water, bull reds will sound and turn sideways like jacks. Use the old billfish charter captain's trick and turn the fish rapidly and repeatedly 360 degrees, using the electric motor. You make the fish feel like you're dragging it around in circles, and not the other way around. It feels like you have control, so it's inclined to change tactics, maybe head for the surface. SB

A trolling motor, background, helped chase down this thick winter red.

CHAPTER 12

Deepwater Reds

Red drum are primarily estuarine species. But at certain times of the year they move into deep inlets and passes, and even to offshore reefs. When targeting reds in deeper water, you trade out the light tackle and leave stealth mode. Steel anchors and lead weights become the most important weapons in the arsenal. Medium-heavy spin or conventional rods and reels also get the nod. Fly casting for deepwater reds, while masochistic, isn't impossible. Ten- to 12-weight rods are loaded up with heavy sinking lines and the "dredging" begins with heavy Clouser Minnows, typically.

Fishing for reds in deep water is literally heavy lifting. A fish may make one or two horizontal runs. But fish caught in deep water fight like jacks and bulldog and circle. Make sure your knots and back are up to the task.

Most deepwater reds are either spawning or getting ready to spawn. Catch and release as gently as possible.

Lead-head jig-type lures such as the
D.O.A. TerrorEyz bounce bottom well
in deep, swift-moving channels.

Reds—Down and Dirty

In late summer and fall, as water temperatures begin to fall into the mid-70s, schools of bull reds migrate close to the beaches, inlet mouths and deep passes. Notable spawning aggregations are in the

Spawning begins as early as late August and runs right through the month of November. The best bull redfish opportunities come during the spawn. Here, redfish weighing from 12 to well over 50 pounds may congregate in a very small area.

Anchoring at the end of jetties is one of the best ways to get in position. There are often deep holes just outside inlets and passes, formed by the strong tides. One of the best methods is to fish a live finger mullet smack on the bottom with medium-heavy spinning

Sometimes red snapper fishermen hook something a little stronger than a "genuine" and figure it's a grouper when up comes a redfish.

Stout conventional gear, downriggers and high-gunneled boats are appropriate for this game.

Jacksonville, Florida area; several Northwest Florida passes; Alabama's Dixey Bar; off Venice, Louisiana; Savannah, Georgia; Charleston, South Carolina; the Outer Banks of North Carolina, and off too many Texas passes to name. Spawning typically takes place during a full moon and at night.

or conventional tackle. In many places, an annual fall mullet run coincides with spawning season, so catching bait isn't hard. A ½-ounce, curly-tail jig is great for prospecting. The fall presents anglers with opportunities to catch trophy redfish on light tackle and fly gear as well.

Deepwater Structure

Look for bull reds to hold close to menhaden and mullet schools during late summer. That means along rock jetties, inlet mouths, deep sloughs and live bottom. Jetty rocks are perhaps the most common place to find reds in deep water. During the slower tide stages, redfish school in deep holes and along portions of the jetty rocks that have been destroyed by storms.

Bull redfish will also hold at nearshore live bottoms and humps. Mud humps associated with the Mississippi Delta can be nothing short of spectacular.

"I enjoyed one of my better days of redfishing while casting chunks of cut mullet to an offshore Louisiana mud hump," says Roland Martin, who lives in Clewiston, Florida. "The water was stained, so you really felt like there were redfish feeding on the hump and actually churning up the bottom as they were feeding. After anchoring our boat upcurrent of the hump, we cast our chunks of cutbait back to the mud hump. For the next hour, we caught and released redfish till our arms were literally aching."

Bull reds will also hold at offshore ledges and live bottom and when you catch one, expect multiple hookups. Drift fishermen employing a double rig bottom setup will often catch two big reds at the same time.

Bait and Tackle

The most successful deepwater red fishermen use fresh cut baits, or fresh cut crab. Three-day-old baits do not work as well. Bring along a few medium-action rods and fish on the bottom with a small piece of cutbait, squid or shrimp. Once a whiting, croaker or better yet a ladyfish is landed, cut the fish into

To catch big reds deep, anglers use bottom-fishing tackle reserved for groupers.

When anchoring, make sure to leave enough scope to keep the bow from diving through boat wakes.

▶ Pro Tip Deepwater Tides

The right tide is critical for pass fishing success. In Northeast Florida, Capt. Lonnie Freeman frequently guides his parties to big catches of fall-run redfish. Waiting patiently for several minutes without a nibble, Freeman would announce that the redfish bite would take place in exactly 10 minutes. Ten minutes later, a big school of redfish will move into the deep jetty hole and bend every rod on the boat.

Freeman is tuned into tidal patterns and where exactly to anchor in the deep hole. Especially in the southeastern U.S., look for the slower moving tides to produce the best fall action at inlet mouths, jetty rocks, beaches and nearshore fish havens. Best action typically takes place during the last two hours of the incoming and the first hour of the falling tide. A second choice would be the last few hours of the falling and the first few hours of the incoming tides. SB

2-inch chunks and then barb a chunk and send it to the bottom. Nothing beats cut chunks of ladyfish for deepwater redfish.

Tackle varies depending on depth, current and size of the fish, ranging from 20- to 50-pound test. A 7-foot, 20- to 30-pound class spinning rod is perfect for a variety of deepwater redfishing applications. The reel should hold 250 yards of 30-pound braided line. To rig up, slide a 4- to 6-ounce egg sinker onto the line. Use just enough weight to keep the bait dead on the bottom. Next, run a small plastic bead onto the line behind the egg sinker. A 50-pound-test black barrel swivel is then attached to the tag end of the braided line. Next, tie a 3-foot section of 50-pound fluorocarbon shock leader to the remaining side of the barrel swivel. Finish with a 5/0 to 7/0 circle hook.

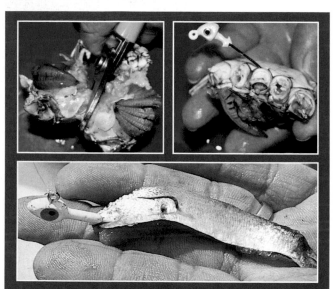

Cracked blue crab, top, is a stellar natural bait and can be fished on a jighead or fishfinder rig. Bottom, mullet or ladyfish strips flutter like the real thing behind a jighead, attracting reds up from the bottom.

This setup and variations of it work extremely well for deepwater redfish whether bait fishing or jigging. When the bite is hot, it's fun to switch from cut baits to spoons or bucktail jigs. Use the same spinning rod used for cut or live baits. Remove the weight and bait hook, and tie the jig or spoon to the tag end of the shock leader.

It is critical to use a jig or spoon heavy enough to make contact with the bottom. In some cases, 4 ounces isn't too heavy. Cast the lure upcurrent and allow the tide to sweep it along the bottom. Keep contact with the bottom while slowly jigging the lure.

Trolling with minnow-type plugs or Drone spoons close to the bottom is also a deadly tactic. In one traditional rig, a 6- to 8-ounce egg sinker is placed ahead of the swivel and shock leader. Next, the plug or spoon is tied to the tag end of the shock leader. Troll slowly through the hole at 2 to 3 knots, occasionally slowing down and speeding up. SB

Reds make a good living offshore, but this one's gut is impressive.

Take your time releasing a bull red. They don't recover as quickly as the puppies do.

Deepwater Reviving

Properly reviving deepwater redfish is critical to their survival, particularly after a long, hard fight. When this occurs, the air bladder inflates and makes it almost impossible to release the hooked redfish without it bellying up.

Fish deflating devices favored by reef fishermen are available at most tackle shops.

The favorite is a thin, hollow brass rod mounted in a wooden handle. The tip is cut at a 60-degree angle and filed sharp. Fisheries experts advise against trying to puncture a fish's air bladder with a knife.

Insert the needle just under the dorsal fin and in the middle of the side while moving it toward the head. Once the air bladder is punctured, gently squeeze the air from the air bladder. Next, place the redfish in the water, while facing the redfish into the current, allowing salt water to run through the gills until it is completely revived. Once the red is kicking strongly, lift the redfish from the water, point it headfirst toward the water and release your catch. SB

A fish is likely to sruvive if deflated properly.

CHAPTER 13

Surf Fishing

Surf fishermen are the one subset of anglers that have always held red drum in the highest regard. For generations, surf anglers have made pilgrimages to the Outer Banks of North Carolina. This is the Mecca of surf fishing for reds, where David Deuel landed the all-tackle IGFA record on November 7, 1984. The fish weighed 94.2 pounds.

At times, there are more anglers targeting redfish from the surf in North Carolina than there are fishing for reds from boats. The same can be said for Texas, some days. When optimal tides, moon and seasons coincide, the surf-fishing action is spectacular.

Surf anglers enjoy a culture of their own, which has given rise to a unique line of tackle and a fleet of eccentric but highly functional beach buggies. These vehicles are usually trucks on gigantic deflated tires. They bristle with rodholders and have huge racks for ice chests. In some places, the culture is threatened as driving on beaches has in places been banned or curtailed.

While the Outer Banks is the most famous surf-fishing destination for reds, the beaches of Virginia, South Carolina and Georgia also offer spectacular "old drum" fishing.

Good timing and strength are needed to load a surf rod optimally for maximum distance. The bottom hand works as a fulcrum.

Redfish in the Suds

North Carolina and Texas are the hotspots, but many anglers target surf-run reds in Virginia, Georgia, South Carolina, along Florida's Atlantic beaches, Florida's Gulf beaches and across the Central Gulf Coast. The waters and tactics vary tremendously among stretches of the coast.

Wave climate primarily determines the location of offshore bars, how close redfish swim to the beach and the appropriate tackle and tactics. Generally, higher energy beaches will have more distant sandbars and a more defined trough or troughs, while low-energy shorelines tend to slope gradually down and across the continental shelf.

The Outer Banks boast the most famous and productive beaches, but this rugged coast is difficult to fish because the barrier islands get hammered by swells. The surf's a little quieter along South Carolina and Georgia barrier islands, but not if a hurricane is pumping swells at them. Northeast and East Central Florida beaches get pretty wild and woolly at times; but sometimes fly casters catch reds in the first trough in millpond conditions. Wave conditions along Florida Gulf beaches vary tremendously, with the toughest surf-fishing conditions occurring from Destin to Pensacola. Alabama's Dauphin Island and nearby sand islands get some surf, and flurries of great surf fishing. Central Gulf beaches, especially in Mississippi and Louisiana, offer serene waters, gently sloping bathymetry and some of the easiest surf fishing for reds in the country. The catch is that in most places you need a boat to get there. The farther south you get in Texas, the more exposed the coast.

Often the bronze forms of redfish are visible in the green faces of waves. So, in most surf-fishing situations, the angler who can cast farthest has the best chance of catching redfish.

"Everyone else spreads out the chances with however many people are on the

Rough surf or bad weather is often better than calm days for catching reds in the surf zone.

Waders, flannels, a trusty surf rod and conventional reel, and huge drum define the Outer Banks surf-fishing experience.

beach, throwing roughly the same distance," explains Bob Eakes, owner of Red Drum Tackle Shop in Buxton, North Carolina.

Most experienced surf anglers keep at least one line in the first trough, especially at high tide. Then the suds usually aren't so sudsy, and baitfish can move in tight and with them come the reds.

"Always keep one short at night," Eakes advises.

In some places, surf anglers keep a rod designed for tournament casting ready with a plug or tin in case reds become visible.

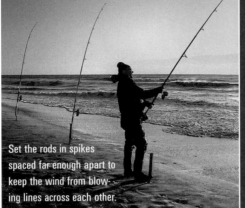

Set the rods in spikes spaced far enough apart to keep the wind from blowing lines across each other.

"I'll catch a fish on it one out of ten times I fish the beach," says Eakes. "But I always take a rod rigged with a 450 Hopkins spoon and keep the line wet and ready to pick up and instantly making a monster cast." Eakes prefers a 2/0 treble hook to a single hook because the single hook will grab the sand bottom like an anchor.

Rods

Until relatively recently, experienced surf casters relied only on custom-made rods. Factory models just wouldn't make the cast.

"I don't mind wrapping rods," says Eakes, "but I'd rather fish. And I can fish more since almost every major manufacturer has a 12-foot rod that will handle an 8-ounce sinker and bait."

Surf rods range from 10 to 13½ feet. If you're really strong, you can go to a bigger rod. Rod size depends on wave energy, current and the distance from shore you need to reach. You want a rod that can throw 4 to 10 ounces of lead cleanly. As veteran surf angler/pilgrim Lou Tabory says, "You want to pop it, not lob it."

Traditional surf-fishing rods are fiberglass; but graphite rods are ever more popular.

Good surf rods have soft tips that aid in the right presentation, but rods must have plenty of power to put the brakes on when fish head for the jetty rocks. One-piece rods are preferable, as they cast farther and there

▶ Pro Tip Northern Surf

Lou Tabory is a legendary New England surf caster who has been making the pilgrimage to the Outer Banks during drum season for decades. Thus, Tabory's witnessed the evolution and had time to refine his preferences. Tabory is a wiry guy, strong and quick, with very good hand-eye coordination and casting skills. His tackle selections run on the smaller side of average.

Rod: G. Loomis 10½-foot casting rod for 2 to 8 ounces. Longer rods can overwhelm all but the strongest anglers and the extra distance is not that much greater.

Reel: Penn International or Shimano Calcutta without levelwind. Tabory prefers bigger reels that hold 250 to 300 yards of 20-pound Sufix Tritanium Plus or Cortland Master Braid.

Sinkers: A 4- to 8-ounce pyramid sinker works well for most fishing, but for extra holding power the anchor (spider or "sputnik") type sinkers with wire legs are best. An anchor sinker is a good choice for an angler who can't cast heavy weights.

Hooks: Owner bait hooks. Hard hooks are important. Better quality hooks will keep sharp longer when dragging through the sand.

Configuration: Fishfinder rigs work well and are very popular. Another good rig is a hook with a short 12-inch leader attached directly to the sinker. Depending on the bait size, use hooks 5/0 to 8/0. Both fresh mullet and fresh menhaden are ideal baits for drum. Remember bigger pieces of bait are harder to cast. Tabory like to cut baits into 1- to 1¼-inch steaks. SB

Incoming tide and surging surf make landing hearty reds an adventure.

brake that helps prevent the spool from overrunning the line. The only brake is the angler's thumb. There were no levelwinds either, so the angler had to be very careful to manipulate the line back on the reel evenly, or a backlash was soon to follow. But because a levelwind reduces casting distance, many veteran anglers still forgo it. Favorites include the Penn Mag 525, Penn Mag 975, Ambassador 7000 C3 and Shimano 700 or 400BSV, Daiwa 20SHW or 30SHW.

Veterans such as Eakes and Tabory advise against braid when fishing in a crowd. It's just too hard to untangle and has contributed to a number of altercations. But surf casters are getting by with smaller, lighter reels by spooling a "backshot" of braid and a "top shot" of 17- to 20-pound-test monofilament. Considering that casts may exceed 150 yards, reels should hold at least 300 yards. The top shot of mono should be longer than you can possibly cast.

If you do use braid, make sure to wind it on at 25 percent of the breaking strength. Otherwise it will cut into itself and backlash. The entire beach will hear the firecracker snap as expensive lead flies toward Europe.

Regardless of what kind of line you use, pay close attention to line level. Buy a simple mechanic's ruler (about 3 bucks) and measure line level. Try starting with the line coming to within ¼ inch of the flange. If the reel is still too hard to control move down to ½ inch from the flange. Higher line level equals a faster reel, which throws farther but is harder to control. Lower line level equals a slower reel that doesn't cast as far but is easier to control. Make an easy cast first to get the line wet before slinging the bait to the horizon.

Spinning reels are commonly used for surf fishing, but are handicapped in terms of casting distance. As the line spins off the spool, it's slapping hard against the guides and creating friction. But the spinning reels are much easier to cast and there's no fear of backlash. In this case, using braided line helps make up for some of the distance handicap.

are no ferrules to "stick" or fracture. Generally, rods in the 10- to 15-foot range will have 4 or 5 guides. More guides reduce the amount of loose line between guides. But extra guides cause more friction and thus reduce casting distance.

"I like to put the first guide 46 inches north of the reel seat," says Ward Woodruff, a Jensen Beach, Florida surf rod builder. "That's about as far as you can go without getting a big bow, which slows your line down and lets the reel get going faster than the line can get out."

Reels and Lines

Conventional (revolving spool) baitcasters dominate the surf-fishing market, because they allow an angler to throw farther. Dating back 25 years, the Penn Squidder was the classic surf-casting reel, and casting one is a real art. The "old school" Squidders lacked a magnetic

Terminal Tackle

You can't fire 6 or 8 ounces of lead plus bait toward the horizon on 20-pound mono without breaking off your terminal tackle. Attach a long shock leader to the main line with a slender knot that will fly through the guides easily. Eakes recommends an Australian Braid knot or No Name knot. The shock leader should be 50-pound test and 4 or 5 wraps on the reel plus the amount of line you want between the tip and the fishfinder rig for optimal casting distance. With the 50-pound shock leader you can really put some muscle behind it, and the 50 stretches like a rubber band to help with distance.

Tie the shock leader to a heavy black barrel swivel. Affix an 18-inch length of leader material (80- or 100-pound-test mono) to the bottom of the swivel; then add a plastic bead, thread on a snap swivel, add another plastic bead and tie the end to another large black barrel swivel. Tie a 2-foot or less length of leader to the lower swivel and affix, with a loop knot, the appropriate hook.

On the subject of weights, the "Hatteras Heavers" traditionally tossed a 4- to 10-ounce pyramid sinker. Even 10 ounces won't hold all the time, and it's very hard to get the distance with so much weight. On high-energy beaches, when the wind, tide and swell direction are all the same, you may actually have to walk with the bait. But a relatively new invention, the spider weight, allows surf anglers to get away with much less lead. These sinkers have wire "legs" that dig into the sand. Says Lou Tabory, "You can get away with a 6-ounce spider sinker in conditions where you need an 8-ounce pyramid sinker."

Use either a large wide-gap bait hook or circle hook. Hooks range from 4/0 to 9/0. Make sure to use a very hard hook and not a light-wire hook, because dragging the hook through the sand dulls it quickly. Keep a sharpener handy.

Live mullet and menhaden are great baits where you don't have to make long casts. Cutbait is overall preferred but it needs to be fresh. Cut a mullet or bunker into 1- to 1¼-

There are a number of variations of the fishfinder rig. One uses a swivel for slide.

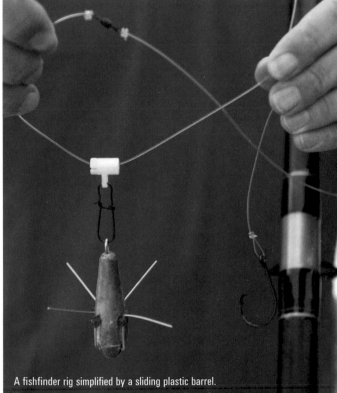

A fishfinder rig simplified by a sliding plastic barrel. The barrel doesn't beat on the sinker and allows for quick changing of sinkers. Circle hook prevents gut hooking and guarantees hookset.

inch steaks. You can't throw a big piece and get any distance. But sometimes it's worth giving up some distance if small sharks and skates are a nuisance. These small-mouthed bottom feeders have a hard time wrapping their jaws around a big chunk of bait. SB

CHAPTER 14

Charts and Electronic Navigation

Paper charts will always be necessary. But the world of electronics has come a long way, baby. During World War II, only the military had access to primitive radio navigation systems. The rest of the fleet used good old DR—dead reckoning. In less than half a century, we've gone from dead reckoning to Loran (LOng RAnge Navigation) to satellite-based global positioning systems (GPS).

Loran is a navigation system using low-frequency radio transmitters; the ship's receiver uses the time interval between radio signals received from three or more stations, to determine position. It worked really well, and some bluewater charter captains still use Loran. But GPS is superior in accuracy and in the affordability and availability of units. The system relies on a constellation of medium Earth orbit satellites that transmit precise microwave signals, enabling a GPS receiver to determine its longitude, latitude and heading. Today's GPS chartplotters offer color screens and space-saving combinations with fish-finding sonar functions.

Charts and chartplotters make learning to navigate an area easier, but patterning the fish takes experience.

Chartplotters provide an electronic aerial view to help navigate complex waters such as Florida's Ten Thousand Islands, pictured here.

Marvelous Machines

Any chapter introducing machines as marvels must begin by pointing out that sooner or later all machines fail. When exploring or fishing waters you don't know super well, always, always carry a compass and waterproof chart of the area. All boaters should take the time to acquaint them-

To get the "Six-Pack" license required for guiding, applicants must pass rigorous navigation tests.

GPS helps a guide run shallow, complex waters while keeping an eye open for tailing fish.

selves with the basics of paper chart navigation. There are several good books on the subject, and most boating safety courses (an excellent idea if you're new to the game) offer at least a rough intro into reading charts and plotting courses with a compass.

Charts

Of course charts are useful for more than basic navigation and those made from aerial photographs may provide great detail of fishing areas. Good topographical charts may show grassflats, oyster bars and mangrove/marsh habitats. Study a chart for deep channels leading back into bays, where the grassflats are located in a bay, where creeks feed the bay and if there are ponds in the headwaters of the creeks. You can also discern broken marsh or small islands. Oyster bars, sandbars and sloughs can also be positively identified.

With knowledge of tides and weather, you can map out a fishing strategy. High-water hotspots may include the backs of large creeks or bays where there are several marsh points, oyster bars, sandbars or even small feeder creeks. During the falling tide, target deeper grassflats or deep sloughs as well as the "highways" that reds use to move from high-water to low-water staging grounds. Keep in mind that wind speed and direction influence water levels on top of tidal movement. On a chart, mark places where you find fish along with tide/time/weather info. Many good anglers keep a logbook of daily observations.

Detailed "hotspot" charts are excellent companions. For example, Florida Sportsman Communications Network offers waterproof backwater charts with popular redfish waters marked on the chart as "RD." Other species are identified on the chart as well. Locations are matched with colored dots, indicating which seasons offer the best action in that particular fishing hole. For example, a red dot indicates that redfish tend to hold in that particular location during the summer fishing season. A star indicates that fishing here for redfish can be excellent all year.

Charts may also mark boat ramps and more importantly, marinas that have fuel available for boats on the water. In many cases, each marina will have a list of its services highlighted, including the sale of gas and diesel fuels. A telephone number also allows fishermen to

Paper charts are still the standby reference for many.

call ahead of time to make sure that they have fuel, and to find out when they open and close. Fuel availability is a major concern when competing in redfish tournaments that require navigating long distances. When long runs are a must, tournament fishermen have to plan the best time to cap off the

Chart chips or data wires upload area maps into GPS units.

boat's fuel cell. Plus, you may need to call a marina for a tow, if you break down.

While navigating, be sure and make notes about the compass headings when navigating to and from unfamiliar waters. Too many anglers have become dependent on a GPS. However, if the power fails, or the unit stops working and you don't have a hand-held back-up unit with you, you need to resort to dead reckoning. Make sure your boat is also equipped with a good compass.

Finally, keep the chart handy, both on and off the water. In many cases, particularly when gassing up at a service station, fishermen will walk right up to you and offer valuable information. It's a lot easier to tell exactly where the fisherman is talking about by looking at a fishing chart. Mark the exact locations, with notes to the best tides, type of cover and lures. Make sure these "treasure maps" are protected from

water by storing them in a dry compartment.

For more information on Florida Sportsman Fishing Charts, visit www.floridasportsman.com. For information on aerial photograph fishing charts, call Standard Mapping Services, (888) 286-0920.

Chartplotters

Chartplotters give a visual chart display, and when linked to a GPS show your position. They can also be used to create waypoints (latitude and longitude positions), and can be part of an integrated system that will show other data such as radar and fishfinders. They sound high-tech, but are downright useful on flats boats and bay boats, even in canoes and kayaks.

Chartplotters are most useful when exploring new waters. When you purchase a chart-plotting GPS unit, you can buy GPS mapping software for a given region. Simply upload software via a data card (a.k.a. chart chip) or wire, and start exploring, carefully. The tracking function lays down a track wherever the boat goes and these electronic stones allow amazing repeatability. Just follow the track home.

While chartplotters help you learn an area, they also help you fish a familiar area more effectively and safely. Often, the best bite occurs right at sunup or sundown, requiring a run in the dark. A chartplotter allows you to simply follow the track you last used to enter or leave an area. That said, the maps on many electronic charting systems don't register exactly with the GPS signal. Fortunately, these maps are usually consistently wrong, if they're wrong at all.

Electronic markers make it possible to locate all those little disappearing sloughs and cuts through outer bars that become fish highways at low water. They can also mark potholes, submerged structure or any other fish magnet.

And when drift fishing, a plotter can help you return exactly to where you found the fish after drifting through or past the school. Some plotters even have built-in tide charts that tell the exact tide stage throughout the day. Built-in depth sounders are very helpful when targeting deepwater reds. Adjust the depth and gain (sensitivity) appropriately.

Running these units isn't brain surgery, so don't be put off by their apparent complexity. Make sure to buy a unit that is "sunlight visible," and color screens are also much easier to read. Think about the visibility when mounting the unit, too, and keeping it away from your line of sight. Units appropriate for backcountry fishing run from $400 to $1,100.

Live Satellite Photos and Chartplotters

Google Earth www.earth.google.com, TerraServer www.terraserver.com, and other satellite map/imagery Web sites allow you to explore an area from your computer. Go to http://maps.google.com/

and click on satellite maps. An aerial map of the United States will then appear. Move the cursor to the location and keep zooming in. Important habitats will show up and are easily identified. Print out the satellite image and use it in conjunction with your charters and plotter. Now, there's an even more high-tech way to do just that. Fugawi offers a Google Earth plug-in for Marine ENC version 4.6. Connect to the internet, select waters and software will pull up and save the corresponding Google images. You can run while viewing location imagery next to your chart. The program works on PCs and PDAs with a GPS connection. SB

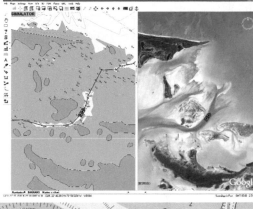

New electronics allow you to split the screen between aerial satellite photos and a detailed map.

The Skinny on Low Water

If you have a boat suitable for pushpole or electric trolling motor propulsion, look for bays that have the numerical number one marked throughout. Large bays with 1-foot depths often lead fishermen to exciting catches of backwater species, particularly redfish. But just because the depth of water is marked "1" don't count on it. In most cases depths marked on fishing charts are taken at mean low tide. So during a high tide, depending on the rise and fall of the tides, you might find five to six feet of water. On the other hand, during an extreme low tide, particularly when the wind is blowing water out from a bay, you could find yourself in less than a foot of water. Be particularly cautious in neighborhoods peppered with oyster bars or emergent limestone. SB

CHAPTER 15

Destination Redfish

No single destination can claim to be "Redfish Mecca." Every angler should experience the time-honored Texas tradition and camaraderie of in-line wading. Every angler should at least once get lost in the marshes of Louisiana, and venture out to the state's sinking barrier islands. Alabama's Dixey Bar may be the most consistent place on the planet to catch a monster red. Florida has more venues than you could fish in a lifetime. Georgia redfishing is a kick in the grass and arguably the nation's most underrated fishery. South Carolina also has plenty of fish and charm. The beaches of North Carolina and Virginia offer the nation's best surf fishing for reds. And redfishing in the Chesapeake is great, if overshadowed by the obsession with striped bass.

The following chapter suggests some of my favorite destinations, but is not meant to be exclusive.

Red drum fare well in a remarkably diverse variety of habitats and temperature ranges. They may be one of the most tolerant fish in the ocean.

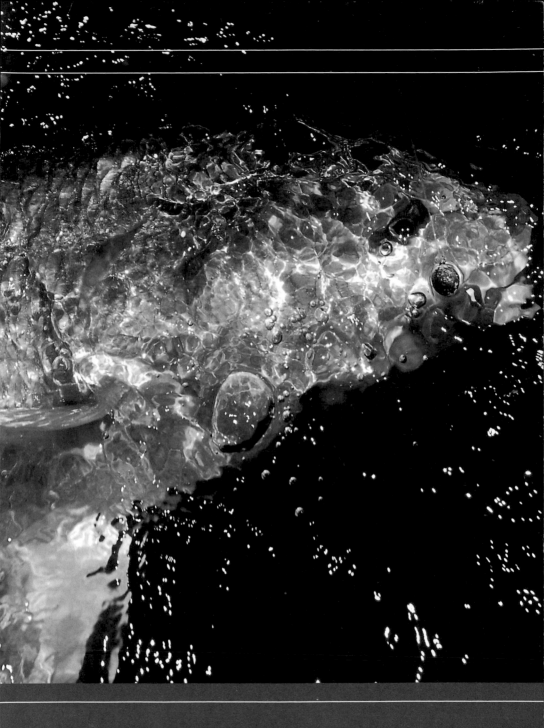

Big shoulders and the distinctive bronze are the draw in 12 states. Reds are funny looking and beautiful at once.

Redfish on the Map

From the South Texas flats to the beaches of Virginia, old spottail is a prized fish.

Virginia

North Carolina

South Carolina

Mississippi

Alabama

Georgia

ATLANTIC OCEAN

Louisiana

Texas

Florida

GULF OF MEXICO

Redfish occur in almost every kind of inshore habitat found in at least 12 states as well as Northeastern Mexico and Cuba. At times, they also dwell offshore, near mud humps on the Gulf of Mexico's continental shelf and on Atlantic shoals and live bottom. Some sub-populations, for example the surf-run fish of the Carolinas and Virginia, make relatively long migrations. Other populations just pop out of a nearby inlet to spawn. Red drum in the upper Indian River Lagoon, Banana River and southern Mosquito lagoon never migrate at all. They live in areas where tide is not a factor and seem content to range five miles or less throughout their lives.

Redfish behavior varies from region to region only slightly. But anglers' tactics vary tremendously. Florida pioneers made an art form out of stalking the flats with one angler poling and the other casting to tailing fish. Texans might as well make wading and blindcasting for reds (and speckled trout) the state's official pastime. Bragging rights for the title of surf-fishing champs goes to anglers in North Carolina, but Virginians catch their share of reds in the suds. South Carolina and Georgia offer the best opportunities to sight cast to reds tailing in the marsh grass, with similar opportunities in Northeast Florida and southern North Carolina. Louisiana Bayou anglers are the kings of the spinnerbait, and Mississippi redfish enthusiasts use a combination of drift fishing and wading to enjoy the fish-rich barrier islands offshore. There's no shortage of places to catch redfish in America, and here are some state-by-state best bets.

No matter where you fish, kayaks can take you skinnier and stealthier than any other vessel.

Beautiful wade-fishing
scenes such as this one
take place in every coastal
state that harbors reds.

TEXAS

Area of Detail

Texas is a big state with a whole lot of diverse coastline to cover. To the northeast, Texas shares Lake Sabine with Louisiana. There the setting consists of marshes and bayous filled with fish. The state also offers lots of open bays studded with oyster reefs and seagrass flats pocked with holes and guts. Top big waters include Galveston Bay, East and West Matagorda bays, Copano and St. Charles bays, Baffin Bay, and of course the Upper and Lower Laguna Madre. The semi-tropical Lower Laguna Madre should be on every angler's to-fish list, but lube up the reels well before you go. The LLM is North America's only hypersaline lagoon. Water depths rarely exceed two feet, and the clear shallows teem with seagrass. The scrubby, desert hills of the mainland seem so austere by comparison.

Texas boasts more coast than you could fish in a lifetime. Venues are almost as varied as they are along Florida's diverse coasts.

Texas

San Antonio Bay

Port Aransas

Corpus Christi

Gulf of Mexico

Baffin Bay

Padre Island

Laguna Madre

Lower Laguna Madre

Brownsville

Texas cowgirl rounds up a red in Port Aransas.

Matagorda Bay

Best Bet

While the Lower Laguna Madre may be the most fascinating ecosystem in Texas, it doesn't quite have the diversity of the **Port Aransas** region. This area has a little bit every kind of redfishing you can do, from a central hub. There is jetty fishing in the passes, surf fishing along the Padre Island National Seashore, fishing the open flats of the Upper Laguna Madre, marsh fishing in Lighthouse Lakes and Packery Channel fishing.

Diversity is the reason why many experts prefer this area even over the Lower Laguna Madre. If one venue isn't producing fish, just try another.

The Lower Laguna Madre is North America's only hypersaline lagoon. You feel like you're fishing in the Great Salt Lake, if the Great Salt Lake had tons of redfish.

LOUISIANA

I f there's a state that's synonymous with red-fishing, that state is Louisiana. Marshes, bayous, lakes, beaches, passes and off-shore humps are absolutely loaded with reds. Top destinations include Venice, Houma,

Area of Detail

Vermilion Bay

Atchafalaya Bay

Capt. Chad Dufrene displays one of Louisiana's finest. Right, Louisiana's immense marsh system.

For its great people and awesome sporting opportunities, Louisiana is a place worth saving.

Golden Meadows, Laffite, Lake Charles, Cocodrie, Hopedale, Lake Sabine and Lake Calcasieu.

However, Louisiana's fecund marshes are disappearing at such a rate that the word "alarming" just doesn't cut it. Flood control and navigation projects constrain the mighty Mississippi River and force it to spew its re-nourishing sediments off the continental shelf. Dredging for oil and gas infrastructure also allows rising sea levels and storm surges from hurricanes to rush right in. Then there are the international challenges of global warming—2 to 6 feet of sea-level rise this century, more intense hurricanes, and the challenges of heat and hypoxia (low dissolved oxygen) in back-waters. All these stressors will make marsh restoration in Louisiana the most challenging engineering enterprise ever undertaken—if it's undertaken.

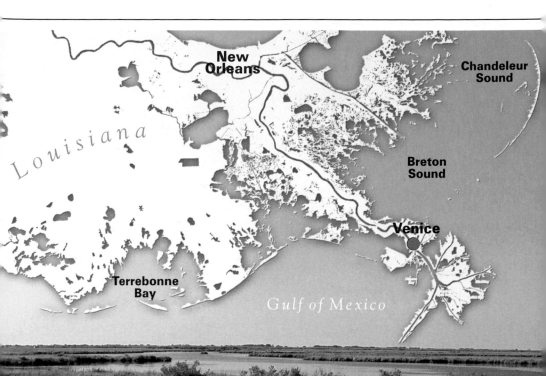

Best Bet

Out of dozens of renowned Louisiana destinations, Venice tops the list. A bad day of redfishing in Louisiana is usually better than a good day of redfishing in other states. Venice is a 90-minute drive south from New Orleans. Numerous guides are available for hire. If you plan on spending a few days fishing here, be sure to make arrangements ahead of time. Since hurricanes Katrina and Rita leveled the place in 2005 hotel rooms are limited and guides stay booked up.

June through November, the back bays, ponds, bayous and rivers offer excellent topwater action. One of the more popular Venice back-bay fishing holes is the Wagon Wheel. The area comprises several marsh ponds, marsh islands and a shallow mud-and-sand bottom. It does indeed look like a circle with spokes from the air. The reds are huge and they love to smash topwaters. In this neck of the swamp, huge redfish are sure to raise eyebrows.

November through late April, some of the best action in the Venice area takes place in the passes and marshes that meet the Gulf of Mexico along the Mississippi delta. Redfish Pass is an obvious favorite. Small shrimp boats anchor just inside the pass and up close to the marsh to clean their catch. Bycatch discarded back into the channel chums up the reds.

MISSISSIPPI

Hurricanes have lashed Mississippi in recent years, but reports of epic fishing soon emerge from even the most ravaged coastlines. Mississippi boasts terrific back-

Area of
Detail

Much of the Mississippi coast has been rebuilt, and smiling anglers are back at home catching reds.

Mississippi

Back Bay of Biloxi

Bilo

Gulf of Mexico

Mississippi redfishing is eclipsed by Louisiana's fame, but is a great fishery in its own right.

country fishing. Backcountry options are plenty along the Pascagoula River marshes and fish best in summer. In most Mississippi marshes, the action peaks in the fall. The Cumbust Bayou marshes, including Bang's Lake, fish well, as do the the northern tributaries, bayous and shores of the Bay of St. Louis. Graveline Bayou really peaks in the fall, as does Fort Bayou. Much of Mississippi's backcountry fishing takes place in "duck ponds," small open-water areas between marsh grass islands. Teal and other waterfowl often pour in while you take aim at redfish. Duck hunters often spot reds tailing in decoy spreads. It's a sportsman's paradise.

Best Bet

The marshes of the Back Bay of Biloxi offer excellent redfishing close to a wide range of accommodations. Black water flows through the marsh system, through a maze of tidal rivers, bayous and ponds. The water is so dark that reds are almost black-backed. But when they roll or tail, fish show up like bright orange footballs. They see artificial lures infrequently, so they feed readily. May through October is best, when the shrimp are in the marsh. The first couple cold snaps really get them chewing.

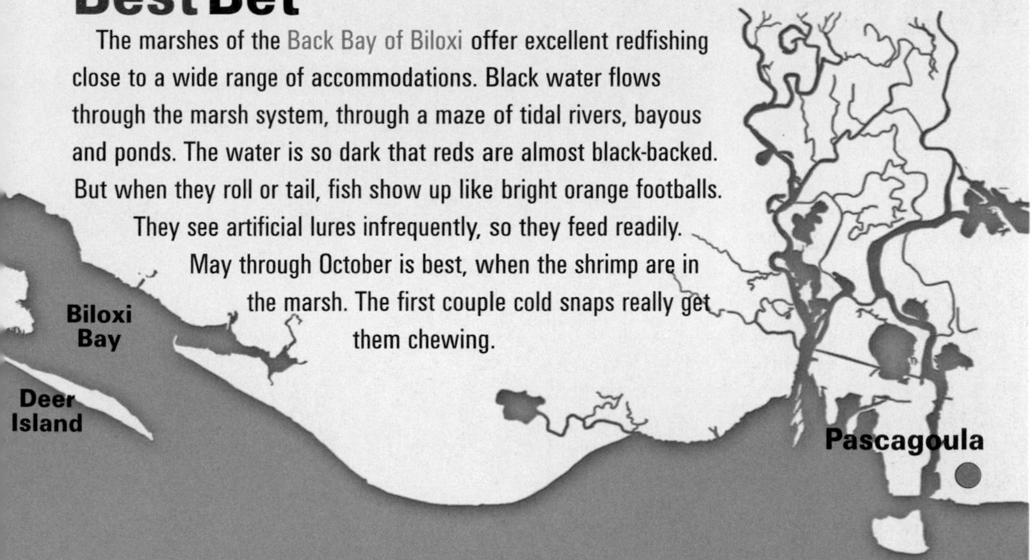

Biloxi Bay

Deer Island

Pascagoula

Mississippi anglers make the run back to a Chandeleur Islands mother ship.

ALABAMA

Area of Detail

For a state with little oceanfront shoreline, Alabama boasts vast and complex marsh systems as well a variety of features in open water that hold reds. Plenty of action nearly on par with Louisiana redfishing can be found in the shallows near Bayou La Batre and Grand Bay. During the summer Mobile Bay is hard to beat. Reds hold just off the marshes in deep sloughs, channels and on the many sunken wrecks in the bay as well. It's fairly deep fishing, jigging mostly, for very large fish.

In the heat of summer and dead of winter, Mobile Bay's deepwater structures hold plenty of reds.

Alabama

Bayou La Batre

Mississippi Sound

Dauphin Island

Alabama's coastline is pretty short, but incredibly diverse. Anglers merrily pursue big reds such as this one on sandbars, oyster reefs and marshes.

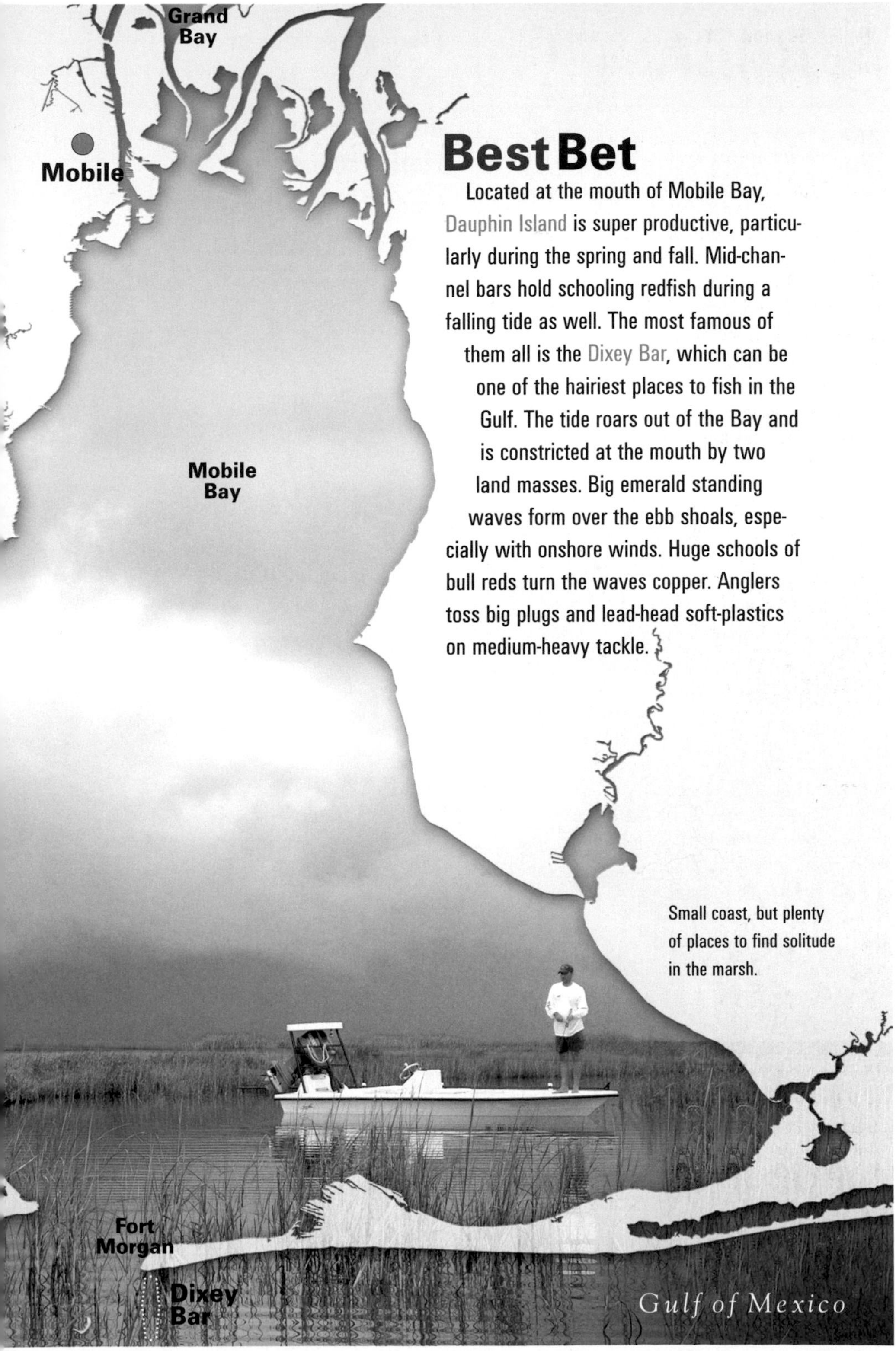

Grand
Bay

Mobile

Mobile
Bay

Best Bet

Located at the mouth of Mobile Bay, Dauphin Island is super productive, particularly during the spring and fall. Mid-channel bars hold schooling redfish during a falling tide as well. The most famous of them all is the Dixey Bar, which can be one of the hairiest places to fish in the Gulf. The tide roars out of the Bay and is constricted at the mouth by two land masses. Big emerald standing waves form over the ebb shoals, especially with onshore winds. Huge schools of bull reds turn the waves copper. Anglers toss big plugs and lead-head soft-plastics on medium-heavy tackle.

Small coast, but plenty of places to find solitude in the marsh.

Fort
Morgan

Dixey
Bar

Gulf of Mexico

FLORIDA

Area of Detail

From grassflats to marsh grasses, mangroves to mud flats, Florida offers every kind of habitat that redfish thrive in.

Florida's ecosystems vary tremendously from region to region, and Florida redfishing varies from place to place. The southern Everglades, including Everglades National Park and the 10,000 Islands National Wildlife Refuge, are national treasures and utterly unique mangrove marsh systems and coastal bays. Florida Bay proper is a world-class redfish sight fishery.

Charlotte Harbor and neighboring Pine Island Sound offer excellent fishing particularly during the spring and early summer. Look for schooling redfish in Catfish Creek, Bull Bay, Turtle Bay, West Wall and Pine Island. Large grassflats and sand holes offer superb redfish habitat. When the tide is up, you can experience exciting action in the flooded mangrove trees.

Tampa Bay, despite being surrounded by sprawl, is quite productive. North of Tampa, the mangrove/marsh systems give way to shallow, grassy coastal bays and marsh grass/oyster reef backcountry, characteristics also found along the Panhandle.

The St. Lucie River estuary and Indian River Lagoon, along Florida's southeast coast, are North America's most biologically diverse estuaries, boasting 800 fish species. The Banana River boasts the famous "No Motor Zone," an area accessible by paddle power only. Some Banana River reds are so old they have barnacles and algae growing on their backs.

The coast in northeast Florida has more in common with the Low Country marshes of Georgia and South Carolina. Big tides flood salt marshes and massive mud flats studded with oyster reefs.

Many top redfish waters are accessible by cartopper.

Best Bet

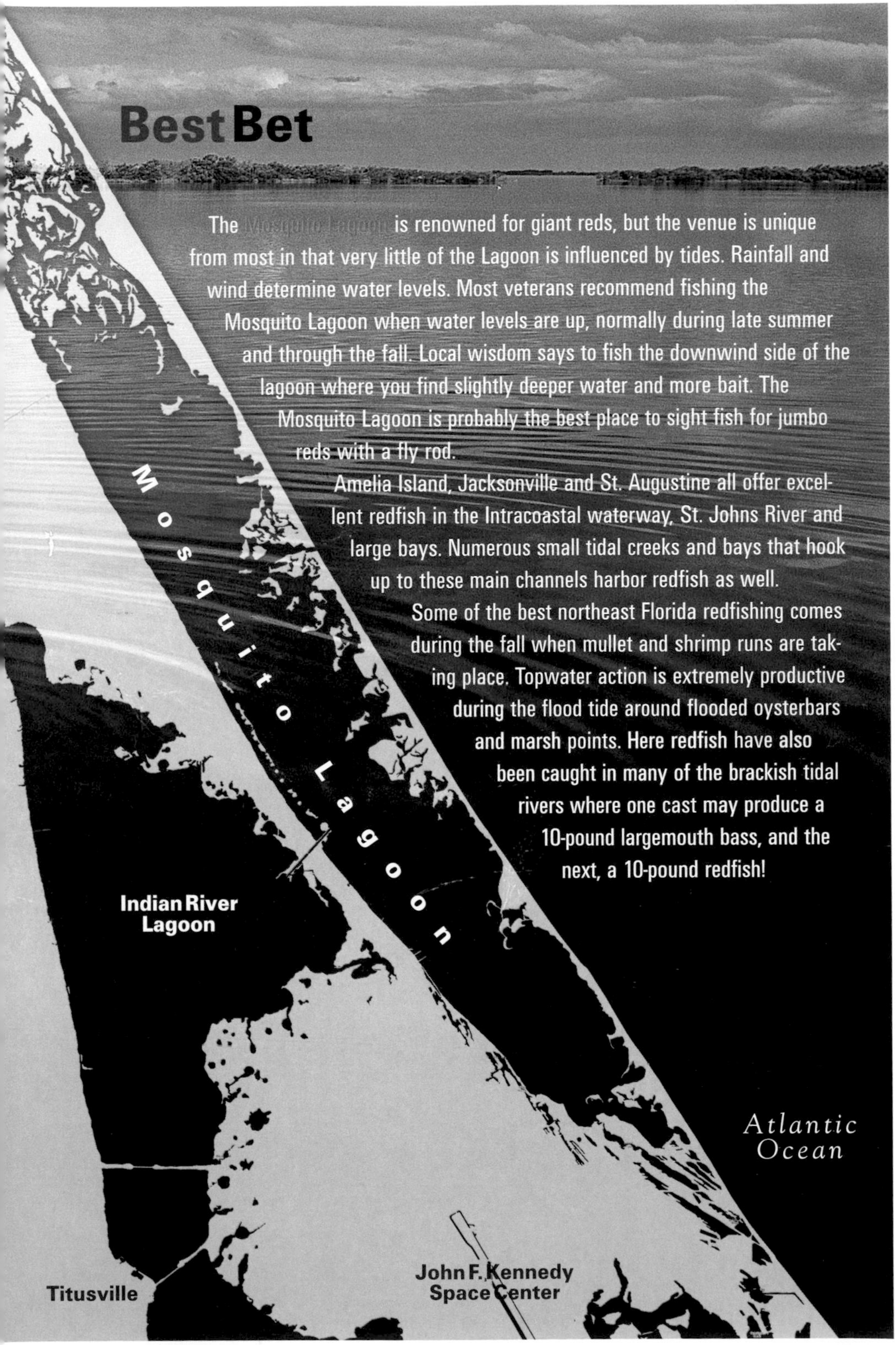

The Mosquito Lagoon is renowned for giant reds, but the venue is unique from most in that very little of the Lagoon is influenced by tides. Rainfall and wind determine water levels. Most veterans recommend fishing the Mosquito Lagoon when water levels are up, normally during late summer and through the fall. Local wisdom says to fish the downwind side of the lagoon where you find slightly deeper water and more bait. The Mosquito Lagoon is probably the best place to sight fish for jumbo reds with a fly rod.

Amelia Island, Jacksonville and St. Augustine all offer excellent redfish in the Intracoastal waterway, St. Johns River and large bays. Numerous small tidal creeks and bays that hook up to these main channels harbor redfish as well.

Some of the best northeast Florida redfishing comes during the fall when mullet and shrimp runs are taking place. Topwater action is extremely productive during the flood tide around flooded oysterbars and marsh points. Here redfish have also been caught in many of the brackish tidal rivers where one cast may produce a 10-pound largemouth bass, and the next, a 10-pound redfish!

Mosquito Lagoon

Indian River Lagoon

Atlantic Ocean

Titusville

John F. Kennedy Space Center

GEORGIA

Most of Georgia's salt marshes and barrier islands are protected from development. The mazes of rivers, creeks and marsh flats offer some of the most overlooked redfishing in America, in some of the nation's most spectacular and pristine coastal wilderness. Thousands of feeder creeks hold redfish during the lowest stages of the incoming tide. Action comes as redfish prepare to move back into

Most of Georgia's coast is protected from development. There's plenty of room to get lost.

Georgia

Georgia's passes and the flats just inside them hold jumbo reds.

Altamaha Sound

St. Simons Island

Jekyll Island

the creeks and flooding marshes.

Top venues include St. Simons Island, Sea Island and Jekyll Island. Fall typically offers the best fishing, when the tides are dramatic and a major shrimp hatch takes place. Huge schools of bull reds weighing from 20 to 40 pounds can be found holding at many of the sandbars located at the mouth of Georgia's Altamaha Sound during the fall fishing season. Cut mullet or ladyfish is the bait of choice for bull reds.

Savannah

Atlantic Ocean

Dramatic fall tides flood the marsh. Reds pile on to feed on fiddler crabs, and fly casters follow. It's sight fishing at its best.

Best Bet

Savannah, Georgia is a gorgeous city and the area's redfishing is nothing short of spectacular. From late spring through early fall, redfishing is a "kick in the grass." The most dramatic tides flood the marshes and reds pile onto these shallows for all-you-can-eat fiddler crabs. Fly fishing is the most effective method here, but the fish are shallow and spooky so a very precise cast is necessary. Texas-rigged jerkbaits come in second.

In winter, reds pile onto mud flats into very clear water, ganging up in schools that number in the thousands. The challenge here is to pick a fish on the edge of the school and not cast your line over and risk spooking the entire pack.

SOUTH CAROLINA

Area of Detail

Dramatic tides, huge oyster rakes and one of the best fishery management programs in the country make South Carolina a great destination.

Redfishing in South Carolina is similar to fishing in Georgia. Big tides in spring, summer and fall flood the marsh allowing reds to gorge on fiddler crabs. In winter, the natural algae blooms that stain the water die off, and the shallows get air clear. The fish gang up, and sight casting to fish numbering in the thousands is thrilling to say the least. Top Charleston spots include sections of the Ashley, Cooper and Wando rivers. Other favorite destinations are Georgetown and Myrtle Beach.

South Carolina

Capt. Thomas Maybank put *Shallow Water Angler* regional editor Scott Wagner on this Low Country red.

Beaufort

Hilton Head Island

Bull redfishing is also excellent during the fall at the Charleston Harbor jetty rocks, particularly at the south jetty "Dynamite Hole." Fish the outside of the cut through the rocks while anchored with cut baits or fresh shrimp on the bottom. Other Bull Red Charleston Harbor hotspots include Sullivan's Island and the "Grillage Hole".

Best Bet

Located within a short drive of Hilton Head, Beaufort lacks the kitschy tourist-center feel and crowded waters. Diverse habitat of oyster "rakes," salt marsh, creeks and flats, along with excellent water quality, supply the ingredients for a world-class fishery. The oyster rakes are particularly interesting. At high tide, they are almost completely covered, and the waterway appears to be an open bay. As the tide falls and the oysters get to "burping," the rake rise higher and higher, seemingly out of the earth. You find yourself in a labyrinth of oyster rake "canyons." Reds stack up in the deepest holes.

Atlantic Ocean

Charleston

Edisto Island

South Carolina's many gorgeous rivers offer year-round action.

NORTH CAROLINA

The rivers, sounds and beaches of North Carolina attract redfish aficionados from all over the world.

The Wilmington area, around Cape Fear, doesn't experience quite the range in tides seen in the Low Country. But, spring through late fall, reds push up into the grass and wave their tails in the air. In winter, especially when strong northwesterlies blow straight offshore, reds stack up along the

Red drum hook a lot of North Carolina kids on fishing.

beaches. The surf is dead flat, and boating anglers sight cast to these large fish.

North Carolina is blessed with the 30,000 square miles of watershed and the second largest estuarine system in the United States, second only to the Chesapeake Bay. The watersheds pour into Albemarle, Currituck, Croatan, Pamlico, Bogue, Core, Roanoke and Pamlico sounds. All of these water bodies hold large populations of red drum. The estuaries boast primarily "puppy drum," but Pamlico Sound flats near the Oregon Inlet offer some of the state's best bull redfishing.

Jacksonville

North Carolina

Wilmington

Cape Fear

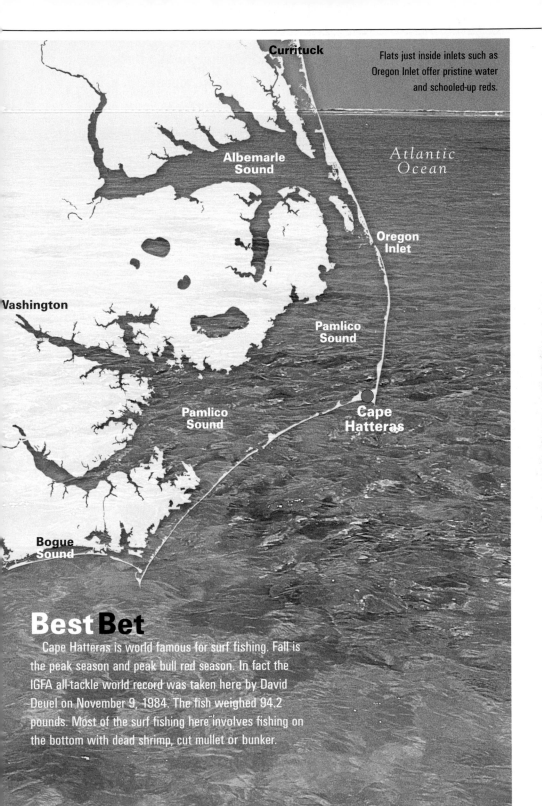

Curlituck

Flats just inside inlets such as
Oregon Inlet offer pristine water
and schooled-up reds.

Albemarle
Sound

*Atlantic
Ocean*

Oregon
Inlet

Vashington

Pamlico
Sound

Pamlico
Sound

Cape
Hatteras

Bogue
Sound

Best Bet

Cape Hatteras is world famous for surf fishing. Fall is
the peak season and peak bull red season. In fact the
IGFA all-tackle world record was taken here by David
Deuel on November 9, 1984. The fish weighed 94.2
pounds. Most of the surf fishing here involves fishing on
the bottom with dead shrimp, cut mullet or bunker.

VIRGINIA

Area of Detail

Although red drum venture into Maryland waters, Delaware Bay and occasionally are caught accidentally in New Jersey, Virginia's beaches and the lower Eastern Shore of the Chesapeake Bay are the northernmost waters where anglers specifically target redfish. The red drum population extends as far north in the Bay as the Patuxent River.

Adult red drum roam the Chesapeake from May through November, and the largest concentrations occur in the spring and fall near the Bay mouth. These are "old drum" migrating in large schools along the beaches. Juvenile red drum also move from bays and estuaries to deeper waters of the ocean in response to dropping water temperatures in the fall and winter.

Redfish forage throughout Chesapeake Bay, but the southeast part of the bay holds the most fish.

Virginia

Backcountry redfishing is just catching on in Virginia. Plenty of water to explore. Left, they say Virginia's for lovers. Stuart Pavlik, looking for love in all the right places, such as the flats inside Lynnhaven inlet.

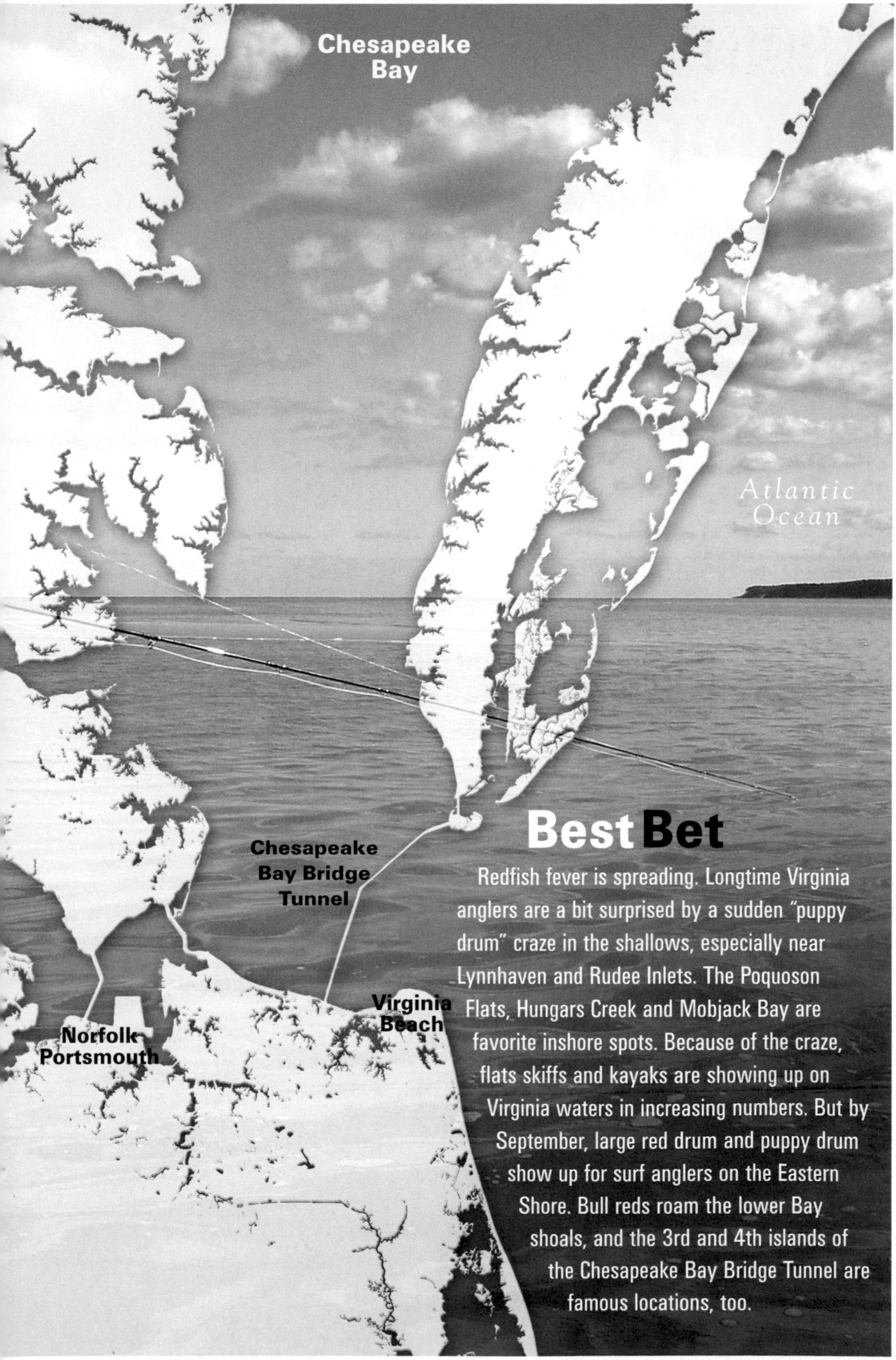

Chesapeake Bay

Atlantic Ocean

Chesapeake Bay Bridge Tunnel

Virginia Beach

Norfolk Portsmouth

Best Bet

Redfish fever is spreading. Longtime Virginia anglers are a bit surprised by a sudden "puppy drum" craze in the shallows, especially near Lynnhaven and Rudee Inlets. The Poquoson Flats, Hungars Creek and Mobjack Bay are favorite inshore spots. Because of the craze, flats skiffs and kayaks are showing up on Virginia waters in increasing numbers. But by September, large red drum and puppy drum show up for surf anglers on the Eastern Shore. Bull reds roam the lower Bay shoals, and the 3rd and 4th islands of the Chesapeake Bay Bridge Tunnel are famous locations, too.

CHAPTER 16

Tournament Redfishing

Redfish tournaments have been around for quite some time now, as far back as 1980. Back then most were single venue events. There are still plenty single venue events, but tournament series such as the Oboy! Oberto Redfish Cup, Texas Redfish Series, and the FLW Redfish Tour draw the big crowds, which throng at the weigh stations. Boats are wrapped like race cars, and some anglers carry themselves with the swagger of celebrity, like NASCAR jocks.

Tournament anglers must understand and adhere to a complex set of rules. For example, some tours forbid an angler to guide in "tournament" waters, hire a guide in tournament waters or purchase information about the area for 30 days prior to the event. This rule helps even the playing field for visiting anglers. Chumming or fishing near a boat that is chumming is prohibited. Wading is a no-no. And of course, every effort is made to release tournament-caught fish alive and in good condition. Hence, there are penalties for dead fish.

Tournament fishing has been a boon for the industry. But some conservation-minded leaders worry about the consequences of such intense pressure and accidental impacts to essential habitats.

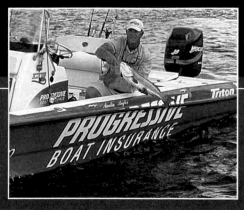

Media exposure is imperative in maintaining sponsorships. Major tournament rules require anglers to pause for the camera.

Life On the Tournament Trail

Because of large purses and sheer excitement, tournament fishing for red drum is growing by leaps and bounds. Anglers can team up with a best friend, wife, son or daughter. Most redfish tournaments are comprised of two-person teams. In most tour-

Florida's popular redfish tournament sites include Jacksonville, Titusville, Punta Gorda, Panama City, Sarasota, Everglades City, St. Augustine and Clearwater. Louisiana venues include New Orleans, Lake Charles, Lafitte and Cocodrie. But without a doubt, the most popular of all Louisiana destinations is Venice. In Georgia, Savannah and Brunswick waters are beautiful and productive. And in South Carolina, Georgetown

Weighmaster calls out the total weight of a team's two fish.

naments each team member strives to catch the heaviest fish possible at the top end of the slot, as close as possible to the legal maximum length. One fish is scored per angler. This format has been adopted by many events.

Exciting venues are part of the allure. Popular Texas tournament sites include Port Aransas, Kema and Port South Padre Island.

and Charleston are also growing in popularity as major redfish tournament destinations.

Redfish tours date back to the 1990s—single venue events to circa 1980. Well-organized, lucrative tours did not emerge until fairly recently. The Oboy! Oberto Redfish Cup formed in 2003, and the FLW Redfish Tour started in 2004. A more recent tournament

Competitors prepare dockside for "blast off."

trail is the newly formed Texas Redfish Series.

All four of these major redfish tournament trails are comprised of two-person teams. Each series awards the team with the most points at the end of the season with a team of the year award. A championship is also held at the end of the season.

Including bonus money for using specific boats, engines, electronics and products, teams can garnish more than $100,000 for winning a single redfish event. Not bad for fishing a couple of days during the weekend with your buddy! Twin brothers Bryan and Greg Watts have won over $300,000 during their seven years of competing in various redfish tournament trails (and counting, at last check).

A Glimpse into the Trail

It was dead low tide. Horsehead Bay on Amelia Island, Florida, was almost bone dry, except for a deep, narrow creekmouth, oyster point and nearby deep slough—perfect low tide redfish habitat in Northeast Florida.

My son, Terry David "T.D." Lacoss made the first cast to the point and began working a topwater plug slowly along the oyster bar. *Boom!* A 7-pound redfish came down headfirst on top the plug.

After a short fight, I slipped the landing net under the fat redfish. We placed the fish on the tournament ruler with great anticipation. The redfish measured just under the legal 27-inch max and so it went into the release well.

"Take the rod, Dad," said T.D., remembering that tournament rules state that an angler can't catch but one redfish. "My fish is already in the release well."

Before the the 2003 Cabela's Jacksonville IFA Redfish Tournament had begun, Florida Fish & Wildlife Conservation Commission (FWC) officials had made it clear that once a

Tournament redfishing involves catching the heaviest fish within the slot. Here an angler makes a measurement.

redfish was placed into a livewell, an angler could not catch a second fish. "Culling," as the practice of swapping out a smaller fish for a larger one is called, was strictly forbidden.

After landing T.D.'s redfish, I quickly caught a 3-pounder. As is often the case in tournament fishing, we had to make a major decision: release the little red and try to catch a larger one, or quit with just over 10 pounds.

We gambled and released the 3-pounder.

Later that afternoon, we fished our way to the very back of Langsford Creek and began casting ¾-ounce gold spoons into flooded marshes. I tossed a spoon up a narrow creek and it wobbled right into the mouth of a 6.8-pound redfish. We headed back to

Jacksonville's Strike Zone weigh-in site, and the fish were big enough for sixth place, with one more fishing day to go.

During the final day of competition, we repeated the same pattern. That day, we released two smallish, 3-pound redfish at the creekmouth and then moved to Langsford

Make it a Wrap

Sponsorship is critical for success. It is simply too expensive for most teams to fund a whole season on the redfish tour without some form of sponsorship. It could cost up to $5,000 per tournament when fishing away from home, including charts, food and hotel rooms. The entry fee for an Oboy! Oberto Redfish Cup All Star event is $2,500, by itself.

There are several levels of sponsorship, beginning with a discounted boat, motor and trailer or fishing tackle. The next level includes a memo-billed boat, trailer and motor. This means a manufacturer or dealership allows you to use a boat free or allows you to use the boat at a serious discount. You don't own the boat, and you're usually required to sell it within a certain time period. Finally, a few elite teams

have sponsors that take care of entry fees and expenses.

Before soliciting sponsorship, first put together a portfolio that includes all of the articles that showcase past wins or publicity. Begin with a local boat dealer. Prove to your local boat dealer that you can help increase their sales. Keep in mind that it is much better for the local dealer to present a request for sponsorship to the manufacturer. Manufacturers literally receive hundreds of e-mails and phone calls per day from fishermen that claim to be the best of the best. However, when a dealer talks with a manufacturer and tells them how your team has actually helped them sell their products, your team will have a much better chance in receiving some level of sponsorship.

Bay boat wrapped with sponsor logos. But when will step ladder companies start sponsoring junior tournament anglers?

Creek. There I hooked a 6.7-pound redfish on a gold spoon and placed it in the release well—a good start.

Four casts later into the same flooded marsh, I hooked a second and much larger redfish. Wondering whether it was legal or not, I passed the rod to T.D. I couldn't put two fish in the well, but was unclear to me as to whether an angler had to hook and land a fish, or just land it.

The big red rolled, kicked and thrashed in the marsh, attempting desperately to shake the spoon. While T.D. kept the rod deeply bent, I powered into the marsh with the electric motor on full speed. With arms outstretched, I swooped the redfish. It was a keeper.

Back at the weigh-in, the two-day catch held up for first place honors, barely edging out long time friends, Larry Miniard and Keith Reiger.

However, before Team Lacoss could claim the $40,000 prize, we had to pass a lie detector test.

With all of the culling regulations, I was still a little uncertain if we had broken any rules. The officials decided that we had acted in the spirit of the rules as we never had more than two redfish landed by one angler in the release well at one time.

The following year, Team Lacoss came in a close second. During the tournament seasons, we broke several records while winning the ESPN Inaugural Cabela's IFA Cocodrie Louisiana Redfish Cup. But the highlight of my fishing career was winning at home, with my son. SB

Finally, once you have some level of sponsorship, make sure that you keep your sponsors updated with any success you have enjoyed on the redfish tour. More importantly, send them photos of big catches with their product in the background.

www.ohboyoberto.com

CHAPTER 17

Conservation

Good fisheries management and good habitat protection are the two essential keys to having plenty of fish and marine life out there. All anglers can help to achieve and maintain these goals. In fact, private citizens are crucial to the effort because government programs often are compromised by special interest influences and by shortfalls in budgets.

We simply have to pitch in, or we lose the public resource and our enjoyment of it.

Fortunately, more and more anglers and their organizations are standing tall to demand effective management and reductions of pollution and habitat loss.

It's heartening to look back on dozens of victories we've achieved over the past four decades. Few of them have been as significant as the Redfish Victory covered here.

Of course, the conservation fight goes on. Let's all dig in.

Being involved in conservation work is one of the defining characteristics of a true sportsman.

Thanks to efforts by the Coastal Conservation Association and predecessor redfish organizations, scenes such as this netting operation are in most places past history.

Gamefish Status Didn't Come Easy

By Karl Wickstrom
Founder, *Florida Sportsman* magazine

The great angling for redfish we enjoy didn't just happen. It was no stroke of luck out of the blue.

In Florida, which now hosts a record amount of redfishing, success came only after a long and bitter conservation war. Many younger fishermen know little or nothing of

Political power of fishermen showed up as never before and turned the tide for redfish.

the tumultuous days in the '80s when recreational and commercial forces squared off by the hundreds before government bureaucrats who had long been under the influence of market lobbyists.

Finally, after a second packed-house hearing before the governor and cabinet, Florida approved gamefish status for the reds, taking them off meat counters in 1989.

It was a huge fisheries conservation victory that set the stage for many more reforms. The Redfish Victory should be embedded in our collective memory of how we defeated (on a state level at least) over-exploitation and recognized the higher value of spreading non-sale catches equally among all citizens.

On a personal note, I won't forget speaking before the cabinet when I heard loud cheers and applause coming from outside the crammed auditorium. It turned out that more than a hundred anglers were out in the hallways listening on a speaker system. (They weren't cheering for me, certainly. They were insistent more than ever that the fish be man-

> Politicians think in two- and four-year spans. Anglers think in terms of generations. For the kids' sakes, get involved.

aged for all.)

A long-term cabinet aide said the redfish turnout was the biggest crowd ever to appear before the top officials, who at the time were required to approve decisions by the Marine Fisheries Commission.

The no-dissent vote by Gov. Lawton Chiles and his cohorts was especially welcome because the previous governor, Bob Martinez, and other cabinet members had angrily rejected gamefish status for reds in a business-as-usual gesture to market forces. As that hearing ended, it was saddening to see the leading commercial lobbyist rush to the front and bear-hug one of his cabinet-member friends.

But persistence of anglers prevailed. It is one of *Florida Sportsman* magazine's most satisfying

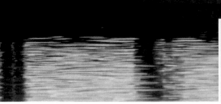

experiences, having called for the gamefish status in the early '80s and helping to found the Florida Conservation Association (now Coastal Conservation Association Florida).

Flashing forward five years from then, *Florida Sportsman* initiated a campaign to ban gill nets in Florida and the then-FCA joined ranks to achieve what is known simply as the Net Ban, ultimately overcoming opposition at every turn from compromised state scientists and political leaders. Prohibiting the entanglement gear saved many thousands of redfish that were netted by accident or design despite gamefish status.

Effective management of redfish actually got started in the state of Texas which had already decommercialized the reds and seatrout and phased out gill nets, all through legislative reforms that did not require Florida's level of political skirmishing.

And now other redfish states in the Southeast are addressing their own concerns about size and bag limits and best uses of the fish.

Rise to protect

The shift toward a conservation ethic also stirs more interest in stocking programs for reds in Florida and other areas, again following an extremely successful hatchery program in Texas that has seen more than 30 million redfish fingerlings stocked in single years. The Texas program is considered a key reason for that state's liberal bag limit of three fish, plus certain takes of oversize fish.

Hatchery raised fingerlings augment native populations. The return on the investment is huge.

To their credit, redfishing leaders in most states have embraced strict limits and in many cases even recommended additional measures designed to keep stocks at high levels.

For the most part, they're more interested in seeing worlds of reds swimming free than piling fillets on cleaning tables (though there should always be places at the dining table for some of these delectable characters.)

This book's author, Terry Lacoss, and I recently caught and released two large keeper-size reds in an hour's fishing just off Fernandina Beach. We both mused about all the years of advocacy and sometimes-agonizing work that made the really good fishing possible, remembering bleak days when the reds were virtually wiped out.

"This is an amazing success story," Terry said. "Lots of people just have no idea what's happened. Now, we just can't take it for granted."

"This is an amazing success story," Terry said. *"Lots of people just have no idea what's happened. Now, we just can't take it for granted."*

A Good Home for Redfish

You don't find redfish in The Bahamas. Why not? After all, The Bahamas offers mangrove shorelines and good-looking flats. So why no reds?

The reason is that redfish must have estuarine conditions to reproduce and thrive.

nurture and protect our estuaries. In many areas, such as the St. Lucie and Caloosahatchee rivers in Florida, the estuarine conditions are ruined by periodic discharges of billions of gallons of tainted fresh water, overwhelming the salinity content and stifling redfish populations, as well as seatrout, snook and many others.

The seven kinds of seagrasses we tend to take for granted, until they're gone, provide food and cover for a wide variety of marine life.

Taking care of the habitat can be just as important as managing the stocks through size

The Magnuson-Stevens Act designates mangroves, marsh grass and sea grass as Essential Fish Habitat and Habitat Areas of Particular Concern.

Mangroves are among the most important redfish habitats, but in places humans have reduced them by more than 50 percent. Inset, volunteers work to change the trend.

Estuaries are vital mixing areas where salt and fresh water join to produce brackish habitats in just the right balance for fish to develop and for seagrasses to flourish. The Bahamas has almost no natural fresh water, and therefore no estuaries.

This important difference is why we must

and bag limits. Addressing both factors is absolutely essential.

So let's all do our part in volunteering for projects such as seagrass planting, mangrove planting and oyster restoration while also demanding that pollution be curbed, and good management maintained to ensure great angling for this and future generations. —K.W.

Top, planting grasses helps stabilize shorelines and creates Essential Fish Habitat. Right, oysters are essential to water quality and estuary health but are mostly declining due to pollution. Fortunately, we have the technology to reduce pollution and restore oyster populations. Bottom, "culch" is deployed for oyster spat to settle on.

REDFISH DVD

How do you spot a redfish in the water? What bait should I use? And how do you get close enough to that spooky fish? If you've asked yourself these questions, this DVD has the answers for you. Join author Terry Lacoss and the editors of Florida Sportsman and Shallow Water Angler as we fish with some of the best redfish anglers from Texas to the Carolinas. We'll show you the tackle, techniques and tips you'll need to catch this illusive gamefish.

FEATURES
- ▶ THE ULTIMATE GAMEFISH
- ▶ RODS & REELS
- ▶ LINES & LEADERS
- ▶ BOATS
- ▶ STRUCTURE
- ▶ LURES
- ▶ BAITS
- ▶ TECHNIQUES
- ▶ BONUS FEATURES
- ▶ GO-TO LURES
- ▶ REDFISH RECIPES

SPORTSMAN'S BEST

REDFISH

DVD VIDEO

Sportsman's Best: Redfish is the most comprehensive DVD on Red Drum on the market today. We cover everything from wading to poling for finding Redfish in mangroves, oyster bars or at the jetties. Whether you're a novice angler or a regular on the tournament circuit, this DVD has something for you.

DVD Executive Producer: Paul Farnsworth
DVD Associate Producer: Matt Weinhaus